FASHION BUSINESS LAW

FASHION INSTITUTE OF TECHNOLOGY

By Professor Frank Lord, Esq. ©

TABLE OF CONTENTS

IMPORTANT REMINDERS:

THERE WILL BE ADDITIONAL TOPICS AND CASES TO BE DISTRIBUTED

MATERIALS FOR EXAMS COME FROM CLASS SO ATTENDANCE IS IMPORTANT REMEMBER: A GREAT CLASS CONSISTS OF GREAT STUDENTS! LET US HAVE A SUCCESSFUL SEMESTER!!!

FM 303 SYLLABUS

PROFESSOR FRANK LORD, ESQ.

EMAIL: frank_lord@fitnyc.edu TELEPHONE: 212-217-4904

IMPORTANT: PLEASE READ CAREFULLY AND ADVISE IF ANY QUESTIONS OR CONCERNS!

COURSE TITLE: FM 303 – FASHION BUSINESS LAW – A practical introduction to the legal environment of the fashion industry. The topics covered here will be applicable to students studying other major academic areas as well!

REQUIRED COURSE WORKBOOK: "FASHION BUSINESS LAW -3rd Edition" (Fashion Institute of Technology) by Frank Lord, Esq. This book is required of all students as it contains the necessary assignments to submit weekly, and the cases that are due for discussion.

AND it is a notebook for students to use during the class, which is highly recommended as a study guide. Exam(s) given during the semester are from the workbook and materials covered in class.

COURSE GRADING: The grading for this course is based on periodic evaluations during the semester. These are the basic requirements to maintain a "B" and of course, for higher grades. Students are able to check their grade status at any time during the semester.

COURSE REQUIREMENTS: Each week, the students will do the required material and have until the following week to submit the assignment before the next class.

IF STUDENTS DO THIS WEEKLY AND SUBMIT THE WORK TIMELY, THEY SHOULD BE ABLE TO GET A MINIMUM GRADE OF "B" upon successful completion of all assignments. The material may be harder to grasp, and fully explain the topics, which may need clarification. This may be difficult to understand especially when briefing and reviewing cases, which can be complex.

There will be additional assignments sent during the semester, which will give students the opportunity to get a higher grade. As stated, grade evaluations are given during the semester. Any issue that prevents attendance or the submission of the weekly requirements, please advise me via email or in class, to discuss. The goal here is to make this a productive learning experience!!!

The supplemental readings and cases will be from actual related industry cases. The idea here is to study and master business and legal principles initially, and then see how they apply to the fashion and other industries.

Again, students will have the opportunity to add cases and concepts that are of interest to the class. These topics can be from any other areas such as social issues, ethics, criminality, textiles, entrepreneurial, business formations, current events, Supreme Court decisions, etc.

SOME EXAMPLES OF LEADING CASES FOR THE SEMESTER! (ADDITIONS TO BE MADE!)

Christian Louboutin v Yves Saint Laurent; Varsity Brands v Star Athletica; Louis Vuitton; Knitwaves, Inc. v Lollytogs, Ltd.; Gucci v Guess; Calvin Klein v Lulu Lemon; Tiffany v Costco, etc.! (There are many more to be added weekly from the workbook!)

STUDENTS CAN ALSO SELECT ANY CASE/TOPIC OF INTEREST!

SYLLABUS AND COURSE OUTLINE
(CASES TO BE ADVISED WEEKLY)

WEEK #1
INTRODUCTION TO THE COURSE & REQUIREMENTS
FASHION BUSINESS LAW DEFINED

WEEK #2
1st AMENDMENT
LEGAL RIGHTS & PROTECTIONS

WEEK #3
INTRODUCTION TO THE LAW
BRIEFING A CASE
JURISDICTION AND THE COURT SYSTEM

WEEK #4
REQUIREMENTS FOR A VALID CASE
BRINGING/PREPARING A CASE FOR COURT
ALTERNATE DISPUTE RESOLUTION

WEEK #5 & 6
OBJECTIVE THEORY OF CONTRACTS
INTRODUCTION TO FASHION & BUSINESS CONTRACTS
REQUIREMENTS FOR ANY VALID CONTRACT

WEEK #7
TERMS OF A CONTRACT/WRITING A CONTRACT
AGREEMENT
OFFERS & CONSIDERATION (TANGIBLE & INTANGIBLE)

WEEK #8
CAPACITY & MINORS
UNEFORCEABLE CONTRACTS
ILLEGALITY OF CONTRACTS

WEEK #9
OVERALL REVIEW OF CONTRACTS
DEFENSES TO ENFORCING A CONTRACT
MISTAKES
FRAUD
UNDUE INFLUENCE/DURESS
STATUTE OF FRAUDS
PAROL EVIDENCE RULE

WEEK #10
THIRD PARTY RIGHTS
ASSIGNMENT & DELEGATION
THIRD PARTY BENEFICIARY
IMPOSSIBILITY OF PERFORMANCE

WEEK #11
DAMAGES
REMEDIES (MONETARY & EQUITABLE)
BREACH
MITIGATION

WEEK #12
NEGLIGENCE/SALES CONTRACTS

WEEK #13	MERCHANTS/FIRM OFFER RULE
	UNIFORM COMMERCIAL CODE (ARTICLE 2)
	WARRANTIES (EXPRESS AND IMPLIED)
	STRICT PRODUCT LIABILITY
	DISCLAIMERS

WEEK # 14	INTRODUCTION TO INTELLECTUAL PROPERTIES
	PATENTS, COPYRIGHTS, TRADEMARKS, TRADE SECRETS
	KNOCK-OFFS, COUNTERFEIT
	BUSINESS FORMATIONS
	FALSE ADVERTISING
	THE LANHAM ACT

| WEEK # 15 | FINAL EXAM |
| | AND/OR FINAL PROJECT |

SYLLABUS SUBJECT TO CHANGE DURING THE SEMESTER

INTRODUCTION - WHAT IS FASHION BUSINESS LAW?

This course is an intellectual challenge to the study of the constantly changing legal principles that are utilized in society today. Students will be prepared for a variety of practices that may arise in both their business and personal relationships. Today, understanding these concepts is more important than ever to have the basic and necessary knowledge to succeed, both on a personal and professional level. However, to effectively do this, it is necessary to understand what the meaning and significance is of "Fashion Business Law?"

First, the following definitions need to be understood, and then combined to fully comprehend what this course will entail over the semester.

I. Law – primarily refers to the principles and regulations established by the Government, which are applicable to all people in the United States and are enforced by judicial decisions. These decisions are based on cases and court requirements.

II. Business – governs commercial matters regulations, restrictions of commercial transactions. This will include contracts, formations, and sales of goods as applicable to all academic areas of study: fashion, entrepreneurship, textiles, product management, and advertising.

III. Fashion – is defined as the prevailing style of dress or behavior at any given time. In addition, the way goods are made and protected.

HOW DO THE ABOVE COMBINE TO FORM FASHION BUSINESS LAW?

Fashion Business law serves to maintain uniformity and order within the fashion industry. It includes the topics of contracts, business organizations, taxes, intellectual properties, as well as other transactions that relate to this specific business.

Another purpose is to resolve disputes, promote and accept standards, protect the rights and liberties of the people, as well as the companies, and to follow the legal guidelines as required by government authorities. Lastly, to keep and maintain its clientele in an ever-changing and complex world!

Thus, fashion law, (also known as apparel law) became a separate legal specialty that focuses on the issues from conception to brand protection. These laws were aimed to assist those clients such as designers, fashion houses, distributors, manufacturers, modeling agencies, retailers, and photographers. The key issues here include but are not limited to intellectual properties (Ex. trademark and copyrights), contracts and business, with many subcategories from discrimination, employment, textiles, modeling, cosmetics, and perfumes.

However, there is the need to understand the basics of the course, which can be applied to any other area of business, and not just fashion! Therefore, an understanding of these issues in all areas has been seriously challenging. It is a field of law that is complicated (to say the least!) even for practiced attorneys. Initially, this means it is necessary to understand the basic legal concepts and then apply them to all industries. **The primary goal of this course is for students of any major!**

Final note: Any business is regulated by the jurisdiction of the state, and federal governments. This means that what applies in the United States, may not apply in other countries. These legal, ethical, and business issues are complex. This class will encompass a progressive process (week to week learning), that will explore all the necessary requirements to understand these concepts and to gain the knowledge to effectively use them.

The Constitution of United States of America 1789

The Constitution has three main functions. First, it creates a national government consisting of a legislative, an executive, and a judicial branch, with a system of checks and balances among the three branches. <u>Second, it divides power between the federal government and the states</u>. And third, it protects various individual liberties of Americans.

<u>How the U.S. Government Is Organized:</u>

- **Legislative**—Makes laws (**Congress**, comprised of the **House of Representatives and Senate**)

- **Executive**—Conducts laws (president, vice president, Cabinet, most federal agencies)

- **Judicial**—Evaluates laws (Supreme Court and other courts)

Note: James Madison (who became the 4th President in 1809) wrote the amendments in 1791, which list specific prohibitions on governmental power, in response to calls from several states for greater constitutional protection for individual liberties.

Dec. 15th, 1791	Bill Of Rights, Amendments 1 - 10
1st Amendment	Freedom of Speech, Religion, Press, Assembly, Petition
2nd Amendment	Right to Bear Arms
3rd Amendment	No Quartering/take-over by Soldiers without permission
4th Amendment	No Unreasonable Search & Seizure of property
5th Amendment	Grand Jury, Right to Remain Silent, Due Process, Eminent Domain, and No Double Jeopardy
6th Amendment	Rights to Trial by Jury & Lawyer given to Accused
7th Amendment	Trial by Jury in certain CIVIL cases
8th Amendment	No Excessive Bail or Cruel and Unusual Punishment
9th Amendment	States cannot infringe on Constitutional rights
10th Amendment	Powers given to the States if not in constitution; *Jurisdiction

July 28, 1868 - The 14th Amendment to the U.S. Constitution, granted to all persons born or naturalized in the United State - "equal protection of the laws.

It stated that no state could "deprive any person of life, liberty, or property, without due process of law; nor deny to any person within its jurisdiction the equal protection of the laws."

July 2, 1964 - The Civil Rights Act, signed into law by President Lyndon Johnson prohibited discrimination in public places, provided for the integration of schools and other public facilities, and made employment discrimination illegal.

The American civil rights movement started in the mid-1950s. A major catalyst in the push for civil rights was in December 1955, when NAACP activist Rosa Parks refused to give up her seat on a public bus.

Title VII of the Civil Rights Act of 1964 is a federal law that prohibits employers from discriminating against employees on the basis of sex, race, color, national origin, and religion. It generally applies to employers with fifteen or more employees, including federal, state, and local governments. (PROTECTED CLASS)

The seventh amendment of the Civil Rights Act of 1964, Title VII, outlines five major protected classes: race, color, religion, sex, and national origin. There are now also protections for physical or mental disability, reprisal and, most recently added, sexual orientation.

June 4th, 1919 – The 19 Amendment- Was passed by Congress and granted all American women the right to vote.

May 17th, 2019 - The Equality Act prohibits discrimination based on sex, sexual orientation, and gender identity in a wide variety of areas including public accommodations and facilities, education, federal funding, employment, housing, credit, and the jury system. The nine protected categories are: age/disability/gender reassignment/marriage and civil partnership/pregnancy and maternity/race/religion or belief/sex/sexual orientation.

Current Members of SCOTUS

John G. Roberts, Jr., Chief Justice of the United States.

Clarence Thomas, Associate Justice.

Samuel A. Alito, Jr., Associate Justice.

Sonia Sotomayor, Associate Justice.

Elena Kagan, Associate Justice.

Neil M. Gorsuch, Associate Justice.

Brett M. Kavanaugh, Associate Justice.

Amy Coney Barrett, Associate Justice.

Ketanji Brown Jackson, Associate Justice.

DECISIONS BY THE SUPREME COURT REQUIRE 5 OF 9 JUSTICES TO AGREE!
This is a plurality decision.

CURRENTLY THERE ARE SIX CONSERVATIVE SUPREME COURT JUSTICES.

QUESTION: WHAT IS THE IMPACT IN TERMS OF ANY SUPREME COURT DECISIONS?

ETHICS v LAW

ARE THEY THE SAME?

Ethics are defined as a moral philosophy or code of morals practiced by a person or group of people. An example of ethics is the code of conduct set by a business (also in a college!).

"Moral principles that govern a person's behavior or the conducting of an activity."
"Legal and medical and ethics also enter into the question and are always an issue."

synonyms: moral code, morals, morality, moral stand, moral principles, moral values, rights and wrongs, principles, ideals, creed, credo, ethos, rules of conduct, behavioral standards, and virtues, dictates of conscience.

Examples of societal ethical behavior can include such things as: respect for another's property; refraining from violence against another; and treating others with civility (policy at FIT!).

Ethics and law are not the same thing. Ethical behavior is not always best defined within the confines of the law. Ethics and the law are not identical. Typically, the law tells us what we are prohibited from doing and what we are required to do in legal situations and endeavors.

Ethical standards are based on the human principles of what is right and what is wrong. The **differences** between them are these:

Legal standards are based on written **law**, while **ethical** standards are based on human rights and wrongs. Something can be legal but not always **ethical**.

Conclusion: all illegal actions are unethical, but not all unethical actions are illegal. Illegal actions involve penalties while unethical actions do not. Laws are legally binding, but ethics are not. Both law and ethics should go side-by-side as they provide the manner on how to act and conduct oneself. Remember, every person is equal under the eyes of the law, and ethically speaking, all should be treated in the same way!

NEWSWORTHY: Thirty-three (33) parents were indicted for crimes that included bribery and racketeering for purpose of fraudulently getting children into college and were indicted and charged with the following:

Bribery - involves an attempt to influence the decision of someone in a position of authority by offering them money or some other benefit (gifts, sex, whatever). It is illegal everywhere on earth, though unfortunately common in some places.

It is unethical because it amounts to an inducement to **disloyalty, taking or using an advantage.** **Racketeering** – generally involves dishonest and fraudulent business dealings. *In addition, racketeering* refers to crimes committed through extortion or coercion. A *racketeer* attempts to obtain money or property from another person, usually through intimidation or force. The term is typically associated with organized crime.

Early **examples of racketeering** include drug trafficking, smuggling of weapons, kidnapping, and counterfeiting. ... Other **examples** of modern-day **racketeering** are human trafficking, bribery, wire fraud, identity theft, illegal gambling, money laundering.

DO THESE CHARGES AGAINST THE PARENTS ILLUSTRATE WHAT IS LEGAL AND WHAT IS ETHICAL? ARE THEY VALID? DO YOU AGREE OR DISAGREE WITH THE COURTS?

ASSIGNMENT FOR WEEK # 2

WRITTEN ASSIGNMENT: PLEASE ANSWER AND SUBMIT IN CLASS.
FIRST AMENDMENT – This is one of the most important amendments that provide certain freedoms and protections to individuals and businesses.

"The First Amendment to the US Constitution prohibits any law limiting freedom with respect to religion, expression, peaceful assembly, or the right of citizens to petition the government."

"The five freedoms that are protected are: speech, religion, press, assembly, and the right to petition the government. Together, these five guaranteed freedoms make the people of the United States of America the freest in the world."

PART I: QUESTIONS TO ANSWER

What is protected under the First Amendment?

What is not protected?

Please read: Miller v State of California 1973

What is meant by a landmark case?

What is the "Miller Test?"

Does this case still have importance today?

What is the difference between ethics and legality?

What are some of the ethical issues faced today?

PART II: Please find any case that deals with the First Amendment (there are many!) and summarize it. (1-2 pages) EX. FREEDOM OF RELIGION!

PART III: PRESENTATIONS - Please THINK ABOUT your topics of interest & submit 2 choices.

EACH STUDENT IS REQUIRED TO PRESENT A FIVE (5) MINUTE PRESENATION ON A TOPIC OF THEIR CHOOSING. THIS IS YOUR CHANCE TO ADD TO THE CURRICULUM SO BE CREATIVE! ONLY AREA OF INTEREST ARE NEEDED NOW UNLESS YOU HAVE A DEFINITE CHOICE. STUDENTS CAN PRESENT A CASE OR DO AN AREA OF INTEREST.

PLEASE SUBMIT YOUR 1ST & 2ND CHOICES! AND I WILL GIVE SAMPLE PRESENTATIONS IN CLASS PRIOR TO THE SELECTION DUE DATE***

PART IV: LET'S RAP! (RIGHTS AFFECTING PEOPLE!)

PLEASE READ THE FOLLOWING CASES

Griswald v Connecticut

U.S. Supreme Court, June 7, 1965

FACTS:

In 1879, Connecticut passed a law that banned the use of any drug, medical device, or other instrument involving contraception. A gynecologist at the Yale School of Medicine, C. Lee Buxton, opened a birth control clinic in New Haven, in conjunction with Estelle

Griswold, who was the head of Planned Parenthood in Connecticut. They were arrested and convicted of violating the law, and their convictions were affirmed by the higher state courts. Their plan was to use the clinic to challenge the constitutionality of the statute under the 14th Amendment before the Supreme Court.

ISSUE:

Does the Constitution protect the right of privacy against state restrictions on a woman's ability to be counseled in the use of contraceptives?

DECISION:

Yes

OPINION:

A right to privacy can be inferred from several amendments in the Bill of Rights, and this right prevents states from making the use of contraception by married couples' illegal. Together, the 1st, 3rd, 4th, and 9th Amendments create the right to privacy in marital relations. The Connecticut statute conflicted with the exercise of this right and was therefore held to be null and void.

Roe v Wade

U.S Supreme Court, January 22, 1973

FACTS:

In 1970, Jane Roe, a fictional name used to protect her identity, filed a lawsuit against Henry Wade, the district attorney of Dallas County, Texas, challenging a Texas law making an abortion illegal except by a doctor's orders to save a woman's life. In her lawsuit, Roe alleged that the state law was vague and unconstitutional, therefore violating her 1st, 4th, 5th, and 9th Amendment rights.

ISSUE:

Does the Constitution embrace a woman's right to terminate her pregnancy by abortion?

DECISION:

Yes

OPINION:

The court held that a woman's right to an abortion fell within the right to privacy (recognized in Griswold v Connecticut), protected by the 14th Amendment. The decision gave a woman total autonomy over the pregnancy during the first trimester and defined various levels of State interest for the 2nd and 3rd trimesters. As a result, the laws of forty-six states were affected by the Court's ruling.

UPDATE: THE CONSTITUTIONAL RIGHT FOR WOMEN TO CHOOSE

- On June 24TH, 2022, the US Supreme Court overturned <u>Roe v Wade</u>, issuing a ruling that upholds a Mississippi law banning most terminations after 15 weeks of pregnancy, and striking down constitutional protections for women to have access. The landmark precedent had been in effect since the1973 ruling.
-

<u>KEY POINTS</u>

- The Supreme Court in a 5-4 decision overturned Roe v. Wade, the landmark ruling that established the constitutional right to choose.

- Roe since 1973 had permitted terminations during the first two trimesters of pregnancy in the United States.

- Almost half the states are expected to outlaw or severely restrict women's rights because of the Supreme Court's decision on a Mississippi case known as <u>Dobbs v. Jackson Women's Health</u> Organization.

- Justice Samuel Alito wrote the majority opinion, joined by four other conservatives. The three liberal justices opposed the decision. Chief Justice John Roberts voted with the majority to uphold the Mississippi restrictions but did not approve of tossing out Roe altogether.

   <u>Five justices signed onto the majority opinion, striking down the landmark decision</u>. They are Clarence Thomas, Samuel Alito, Brett Kavanaugh, Neil Gorsuch, AND Amy Coney Barrett.

   <u>And three justices dissented*:</u> Stephen Breyer, Sonia Sotomayor, Elena Kagan.

   *Dissent: The opinion of the judge of the U.S. Supreme Court, (or any court), which disagrees with the majority opinion.

   Chief Justice John Roberts did not join the majority, writing in a concurring opinion that he would not have overturned Roe but instead would have only upheld Mississippi's law banning terminations after 15 weeks.

   Dobbs v. Jackson is a court case over Mississippi's state law that banned termination after 15 weeks. A lower court in the state struck the law down as unconstitutional because Roe v. Wade had protected a pregnant person's right to choose prior to fetal viability, generally considered around 24 weeks. Mississippi appealed the lower court's ruling, and the case went to the U.S. Supreme Court. Dobbs v. Jackson is the first time since 1973 that the court has ruled on the constitutionality of banning termination before viability.

The court voted 6-3 to uphold the Mississippi law and 5-4 to overturn Roe.

STATE LAWS TODAY

Thirteen states have <u>trigger laws that ban termination</u> with limited exceptions, which go into effect automatically or with quick state action now that Roe v. Wade has been overturned. These states include Arkansas, Idaho, Kentucky, Louisiana, Mississippi, Missouri, North Dakota, Oklahoma, South Dakota, Tennessee, Texas, Utah, and Wyoming.

Alabama has <u>passed the most restrictive anti-abortion bill</u> in the country, promising to jail for 99 years any doctor who performs the procedure*

EMPLOYERS CAN REFUSE TO COVER BIRTH CONTROL

One of the most controversial — and most welcomed — requirements of the 2010 Affordable Care Act was a regulation for health insurance plans to provide birth control coverage free to patients. Some states are allowing refusal of companies to cover birth control under insurance due to religious beliefs.

QUESTION: WHAT WORD HAS THE PROFESSOR DELIBERATELY REPLACED/AND OR SUBSTITUED IN ALL OF THE ABOVE CASES AND INFORMATION? WHY?

Obergefell vs Hodges

U.S. Supreme Court, June 26, 2015

FACTS:

Groups of same-sex couples sued their relevant state agencies in Ohio, Michigan, Kentucky, and Tennessee to challenge the constitutionality of those states' bans on same-sex marriage or refusal to recognize those marriages performed legally in other states. The claim was that the state statutes violated the Equal Protection Clause and the Due Process Clause of the 14th Amendment, and the Civil Rights Act. The Court held that the ban on same-sex marriages did not violate the 14th Amendment.

ISSUES:

Does the 14th Amendment require a state to license a marriage between two people of the same sex?

Does the 14th Amendment require a state to recognize a same-sex marriage performed in another state?

DECISIONS:

Yes, Yes

OPINION:

The Court held that the Due Process Clause guarantees the right to marry as a fundamental liberty, and that analysis applies to same-sex couples in the same manner. Exclusion of same-sex couples would violate Due Process Clause, which in turn, violates the U.S. Constitution. The Court also held that the 1st Amendment protects the rights of religious organizations to adhere to their principles, but it does not allow the States to deny the right to marry for same-sex couples, as it does allow for opposite-sex couples to marry.

R.G. & G.R. Harris Funeral Homes v Equal Employment Opportunity Commission

U.S. Court of Appeals, June 15, 2020

FACTS:

Aimee Stephens (formerly known as Anthony Stephens), worked as a funeral director for Harris Funeral Homes, in Michigan, where she mostly worked as a man. Subsequently, when she informed the funeral home that she intended to transition from male to female, she was terminated. Stephens filed a complaint with the EEOC alleging that the termination was based on unlawful sex discrimination. The EEOC brought a lawsuit claiming the funeral home had violated Title VII of the Civil Rights Act of 1964, based on her transgender or transitioning status. The district court agreed with the funeral home, and Stephens appealed to the higher court.

ISSUE:

Does Title VII of the Civil Rights Act prohibit discrimination against transgender employees based on their status as transgender or sex stereotyping?

DECISION:

Yes

OPINION:

Title VII prohibits employers from discriminating against any individual "because of such individual's race, color, religion, sex, or national origin." Discrimination on the basis of "homosexuality" or transgender status requires an employer to treat employees differently bases on their sex – the very practice Title VII prohibits in all manifestations. The Court acknowledged that in 1964, this would not have been expected but the language of the statute unambiguously prohibits any discriminatory practice.

Masterpiece Cake Shop. Ltd. v Colorado Civil Rights Commission

FACTS:

In July 2021, Charlie Craig and David Mullins went to Masterpiece cake shop in Lakewood, Colorado, and requested the owner, Jack C. Phillips, to design and create a cake for their wedding. Phillips declined due to his religious beliefs, and a cake for same-sex marriage would displease "God." Craig and Mullins filed discrimination charges with the Colorado Civil Rights Commission based on sexual orientation under the Colorado Anti-Discrimination Act (CADA), in a place of public accommodation. The Commission held for Craig and Mullins, and Phillips appealed.

ISSUE:

Does Colorado's public accommodation law compel a cake maker to design a cake that violates his sincere religious beliefs about same-sex marriage violate the 1st Amendment?

DECISION:

No

OPINION:

The Court explained that while gay persons and same-sex couples are afforded civil rights protections under the law and the Constitution, religious and philosophical objections to same-sex marriage are protected views and can be protected forms of expression. The Colorado law at issue in this case, which prohibited discrimination against gay people in purchasing products and services, had to be applied in a neutral manner towards religion. The majority of the Court acknowledged that from Phillips' perspective, creating cakes was a form of artistic expression, and a sincere component of his religious beliefs.

Federal Ruling: As of 2015, same-gender marriage is now legal in all fifty states due to a ruling from the Supreme Court.

UPDATE: Same-Gender Marriage Status

The first lawsuits involving same-gender marriage, also called gay marriage, started in the 1970s, bringing the question of civil marriage rights for same-gender couples to public attention. Many of these lawsuits were unsuccessful. On February 12, 2004, the first same-gender marriage in the U.S. happened in San Francisco, California. Del Martin and Phyllis Lyon become the first gay couple to marry and receive official recognition after being together for 50 years.

On May 17, 2004, Massachusetts became the first state and sixth jurisdiction in the world to legalize same-gender marriage. Following this, opponents of same-gender marriage began tightening marriage restrictions, with several states approving state constitutional amendments specifically defining marriage as the union of one man and one woman.

In 2008, California and Connecticut both legalized same-gender marriage, followed by Iowa, Vermont, and New Hampshire. Up until 2012, legalization came through state courts, the enactment of state legislation, or the result of the decisions of federal courts. On November 6, 2012, Maine, Maryland and Washington became the first states to legalize same-gender marriage through popular vote.

On June 26, 2015, in the landmark civil rights case Obergefell v. Hodges, (see page 11 in textbook), the Supreme Court ruled that the fundamental right to marry is guaranteed to same-gender couples by both the Due Process Clause and the Equal Protection Clause of the Fourteenth Amendment to the United States Constitution. However, not all state legislatures are abiding by this decision and have enacted constitutional or statutory bans on same-gender marriage, known as the "Defense of Marriage" Acts. Thirteen of the 50 U.S. states still have a ban on same-gender marriage.

Same-Gender Marriage by State

The following 13 states have not legalized or recognized same-gender marriage: Arkansas, Georgia, Kentucky, Louisiana, Michigan, Mississippi, Missouri, Nebraska, North Dakota, Ohio, South Dakota, Tennessee, and Texas. Thirty-seven states have legalized gay marriage, with restrictions in Kansas, Missouri, and Alabama.

The following 37 states (and the District of Columbia) have legalized same-gender marriage: Alabama (2015), Alaska (2014), Arizona (2014), California (2008), Colorado (2014), Connecticut (2008), Delaware (2013), District of Columbia (2010), Florida (2014), Hawaii (2013), Idaho (2014), Illinois (2014), Indiana (2014), Iowa (2009), Kansas (2015), Maine (2012), Maryland (2012), Massachusetts (2004), Minnesota (2013), Montana (2014), Nevada (2014), New Hampshire (2010), New Jersey (2013), New Mexico (2013), New York (2011), North Carolina (2014), Oklahoma (2014), Oregon (2014), Pennsylvania (2014), Rhode Island (2013), South Carolina (2014), Utah (2014), Vermont (2009), Virginia (2014), Washington (2012), West Virginia (2014), Wisconsin (2014), and West Virginia (2014).

Respect for Marriage Act – December 13, 2022

This act provides statutory authority for same-sex and interracial marriages.

Specifically, the act replaces provisions that define, for purposes of federal law, *marriage* as between a man and a woman and *spouse* as a person of the other sex with provisions that recognize any marriage between two individuals that is valid under state law. (The Supreme Court held that the current provisions were unconstitutional in *United States v. Windsor* in 2013.

The act also replaces provisions that do not require states to recognize same-sex marriages from other states with provisions that prohibit the denial of full faith and credit or any right or claim relating to out-of-state marriages on the basis of sex, race, ethnicity, or national origin. (The Supreme Court held that state laws barring same-sex marriages were unconstitutional in *Obergefell v. Hodges* in 2015; the Court held that state laws barring interracial marriages were unconstitutional in *Loving v. Virginia* in 1967.) The act allows the Department of Justice to bring a civil action and establishes a private right of action for violations.

The act does not (1) affect religious liberties or conscience protections that are available under the Constitution or federal law, (2) require religious organizations to provide goods or services to formally recognize or celebrate a marriage, (3) affect any benefits or rights that do not arise from a marriage, or (4) recognize under federal law any marriage between more than two individuals.

QUESTION: WHAT WORD HAS THE PROFESSOR DELIBERATELY REPLACED/AND OR SUBSTITUED IN ALL OF THE ABOVE CASES AND INFORMATION? WHY?

United States v. Windsor (2013)

This case was one of the major precursors to marriage equality. The Court decided to eliminate the portion of the Defense of Marriage Act (DOMA) of 1996 that defined marriage as a "legal union between one man and one woman as husband and wife." The case considered the situation of Edith Windsor and Thea Spyer, who were married in Canada before moving to New York, a state that recognized their marriage. After Spyer passed away, Windsor's attempted to claim a tax exemption for surviving spouses — only to be blocked by DOMA. In a 5-4 vote, Supreme Court ruled that DOMA violates due process and equal protection principles and ordered the United States to refund Windsor's taxes.

Recent update June 30, 2023 - In a blow to LGBT rights, the U.S. Supreme Court's conservative majority on Friday ruled that the constitutional right to free speech allows certain businesses to refuse to provide services for same-sex weddings, a decision that the dissenting liberal justices called a "license to discriminate."

How Can We Promote Equality and Diversity?

Gender equality occurs when people of all genders have equal rights, responsibilities, and opportunities. Everyone is affected by gender inequality -

women, men, trans and gender diverse people, children, and families. It influences people of all ages and backgrounds.

Ex. Gender-fair language (GFL) aims at reducing gender stereotyping and discrimination.

- Folks/everybody/people instead of guys or ladies/gentleman
- Humankind instead of mankind
- People instead of man/men and woman/women
- Members of Congress or Congressional Representatives, instead of congressmen
- Councilperson instead of councilman/councilwoman
- Chair/Chairperson instead of Chairman
- Executive or Businessperson instead of businessman
- First-year student instead of freshman
- Machine-made, synthetic, or artificial instead of man-made
- Parent or Pibling instead of mother/father
- Child instead of son/daughter
- Sibling instead of sister/brother
- Nibling instead of niece/nephew
- Partner, significant other, or spouse instead of girlfriend/boyfriend or wife/husband
- Flight attendant instead of steward/stewardess
- Salesperson or sales representative instead of salesman/saleswoman
- Server instead of waiter/waitress
- Police Officer instead of policeman
- Firefighter instead of fireman
- Non-binary is an umbrella term to describe people who identify with a gender outside of the gender binary of male and female.

A non-binary person simply identifies with a gender that is not male or female.

Ex. Gender fluid –

Between two or more gender identities.

Supreme Court Cases in Women's Rights
U.S. SUPREME COURT AKA "SCOTUS"

Muller v. Oregon (1908)

SCOTUS upheld an Oregon state law-limiting women to working no more than ten hours a day. Three years earlier, in *Lochner v. New York,* the Court had ruled that a state could not restrict the working hours of men, on the grounds that doing so would infringe on their right as workers to make their own working arrangements with employers. In this case, it held that this right was outweighed by the state's interest in protecting women.

The case featured what is now known as the "Brandeis brief," written to support Oregon's case by future justice Louis Brandeis. It contained two pages discussing legal issues, and 110 pages of data providing evidence that long working hours had negative effects on the "health, safety, morals, and general welfare of women." This was the first time such data had been used in a Supreme Court case to demonstrate a reasonable basis for a state law.

Adkins v. *Children's Hospital* (1923)

SCOTUS struck down a federal law establishing a minimum wage for women in Washington, D.C. While the Court continued to hold that states could regulate the amount of time worked by women, they held that this was different from regulating the wages they could make. In the latter regard, they were held to have the right to make any arrangements they pleased, just like men.

This case pitted opposing groups of women's rights activists against one another, with one side fighting for women to receive increased protection, and the other wanting women to be on an equal footing with men.

West Coast Hotel Co. v. *Parrish* (1937)

SCOTUS overturned *Adkins* v. *Children's Hospital,* upholding a Washington state law, which established minimum wages for women and minors.

Phillips v. *Martin Marietta Corp.* (1971)

In a *per curiam* *decision, SCOTUS ruled that employers could not refuse to hire women with pre-school children while hiring men with such children.

*A per curiam decision is **a court opinion issued in the name of the Court rather than specific judges.** Most decisions on the merits by the courts take the form of one or more opinions written and signed by individual justices. Often, other judges/justices will join these opinions.

Reed v. *Reed* (1971)

SCOTUS struck down an Illinois law giving preference to a male seeking to administrate an estate over an equally entitled female. This case concerned a set of separated parents whose adopted son had died without a will. Both sought to administrate the deceased's estate; following the law, a lower court had placed the father in charge. The Supreme Court ruled that men and women could be treated differently only when there was some reasonable and relevant cause for doing so; while the Illinois law simplified judicial proceedings, arbitrarily giving preference to men over women was "to make the very kind of arbitrary legislative choice forbidden by the Equal Protection Clause of the Fourteenth Amendment."

Eisenstadt v. *Baird* (1972)

SCOTUS struck down a Massachusetts law banning the distribution of contraceptives to unmarried persons. The right to privacy established in *Griswold* v. *Connecticut* was now established as extending to *individuals,* married or single, rather than existing only between partners in a marriage.

Pittsburgh Press Co. v. *Pittsburgh Commission on Human Relations* (1973)

SCOTUS upheld a Pittsburgh ordinance making it illegal to indicate a gender requirement in most job postings. The *Pittsburgh Press* newspaper had "help wanted" listings in three columns: "Jobs—Male Interest," "Jobs—Female Interest," and "Male-Female." A lower court held that this violated Pittsburgh law, and the newspaper appealed on First Amendment grounds, claiming that this law violated the freedom of the press. The Supreme Court ruled that as the ads were commercial speech, and especially as the discrimination itself was illegal, free speech rules did not apply to them or to their classification by the newspaper.

Doe v. *Bolton* (1973)

SCOTUS established *Roe* v. *Wade* overturned Georgia's abortion law on the same day. Among the law's restrictions were the requirements that the abortion take place in an accredited hospital, that patient obtain the approval of three physicians *and* the hospital's abortion committee, and that the patient be a resident of Georgia. These restrictions were found to infringe upon the rights of the patient and those of her primary physician.

Harris v. *McRae* (1980)

SCOTUS upheld a law barring the use of Medicaid funds for abortions, except in specific cases. The Hyde Amendment allowed the funding of abortions in cases when the mother's life was in danger, and in cases of rape or incest. The Court held that a woman's right to terminate a pregnancy did not entitle her to receive government funding for that choice.

International Union, UAW v. *Johnson Controls, Inc.* (1991)

SCOTUS held that a battery manufacturer could not bar fertile women from jobs involving exposure to lead, despite the potential for fetuses being harmed by lead poisoning. It found that this was a case of sex discrimination, as no similar policy was in place for fertile men, despite the potential for dangerous effects on the male reproductive system. Furthermore, childbearing concerns were irrelevant to employees' abilities to conduct the functions of their jobs, which would be the only legitimate reason for discrimination.

Webster v. *Reproductive Health Services* (1989)

SCOTUS upheld several restrictions placed on abortion in Missouri. It found that the state could prohibit the use of state employees or facilities for abortions not necessary to save the mother's life; prohibit the use of public funds, employees, or facilities to encourage or counsel a woman have an abortion for non-life-saving purposes; and require physicians to perform a test to see whether a fetus is viable, if they have reason to believe that the mother is at least 20 weeks pregnant. The first two were found to be essentially the same as the restrictions on public funding upheld in *Harris* v. *McRae,* while the viability test was found not to be in violation of *Roe*.

Planned Parenthood v. *Casey* (1992)

SCOTUS upheld several Pennsylvanian abortion restrictions, while striking down the requirement for notifying husbands. It held that it was legal to require doctors to provide women with information on the potential risks associate with abortions at least 24 hours before the procedure was performed, and to require a minor seeking an abortion to obtain either the consent of one of her parents or a judicial bypass. Under Pennsylvania law, these requirements did not apply in cases of a "medical emergency." The plurality opinion, written by Sandra Day O'Connor, rejected the rigid trimester distinctions of *Roe* in which a state's interest in potential life could not be the basis for regulation until the third trimester. Instead, it held that regulations on abortion could not impose an "undue burden," which, in this case, applied only to spousal notification.

United States v. *Virginia* (1996)

SCOTUS rules against the Virginia Military Institute's (VMI) male-only admissions policy. VMI was the only public institution left in the United States with a male-only bias and would have not been eligible to receive federal monies had it remained all males.

Nevada Dept. of Human Resources v. *Hibbs* (2003)

SCOTUS rules that states can be sued in federal court for violations of the Family Leave Medical Act.

Jackson v. *Birmingham Board of Education* (2005)

SCOTUS rules that Title IX, which prohibits discrimination based on sex, also inherently prohibits disciplining someone for complaining about sex-based discrimination. It further holds that this is the case even when the person complaining is not among those being discriminated against.

IMPORTANT CASES IN THE HISTORY OF CIVIL RIGHTS

Dred Scott v Sanford (1857)

Decreed a slave was his master's property and African Americans were not citizens; struck down the Missouri Compromise as unconstitutional.

Civil Rights Cases (1883)

A number of cases are addressed under this Supreme Court decision. Decided that the Civil Rights Act of 1875 (the last federal civil rights legislation until the Civil Rights Act of 1957) was unconstitutional. Allowed private sector segregation.

Plessy v. Ferguson (1896)

The Court stated that segregation was legal and constitutional as long as "facilities were equal"—the famous "separate but equal" segregation policy.

Powell v. Alabama (1932)

The Supreme Court overturned the "Scottsboro Boys'" convictions and guaranteed counsel in state and federal courts.

Shelley v. Kraemer (1948)

The justices ruled that a court may not constitutionally enforce a "restrictive covenant" which prevents people of certain race from owning or occupying property.

Brown v. Board of Education of Topeka (1954)

Reversed *Plessy v. Ferguson* "separate but equal" ruling. "[S]egregation [in public education] is a denial of the equal protection of the laws."

Heart of Atlanta Motel, Inc. v. United States (1964)

This case challenged the constitutionality of the Civil Rights Act of 1964. The court ruled that the motel had no right "to select its guests as it sees fit, free from governmental regulation."

Loving v. Virginia (1967)

This decision ruled that the prohibition on interracial marriage was unconstitutional. Sixteen states that still banned interracial marriage at the time were forced to revise their laws.

Regents of the University of California v. Bakke (1978)

The decision stated that affirmative action was unconstitutional in cases where the affirmative action program used a quota system.

Grutter v. Bollinger (2003)

The decision-upheld affirmative action's constitutionality in education, as long it employed a "highly individualized, holistic review of each applicant's file" and did not consider race as a factor in a "mechanical way."

NOTES AND ASSIGNMENTS

ASSIGNMENT WEEK #3

PLEASE DEFINE THE FOLLOWING VOCABULARY TERMS FROM THE BOOK ALSO, THINK OF AN EXAMPLE OR WHAT THE SIGNIFICANCE OF THE TERM IS!

JURISDICTION

DEFINITION: _____

_____

_____

EXAMPLE: _____

_____

_____

SUBJECT MATTER JURISDICTION

DEFINITION: _____

_____

_____

EXAMPLE: _____

_____

_____

PERSONAL JURISDICTION

DEFINITION: _____

_____

_____

EXAMPLE: _____

_____

_____

COURTS OF LIMITED JURISDICTION

DEFINITION: _____

_____

_____

EXAMPLE: _____

_____

_____

COURTS OF GENERAL JURISDICTION

DEFINITION: _____

_____

_____

EXAMPLE: _____

_____

_____

COURT OF APPEALS

DEFINITION: _____

_____

_____

EXAMPLE: _____

_____

_____

STATE SUPREME COURT

DEFINITION: _____

_____

_____

EXAMPLE: _____

_____

_____

FEDERAL DISTRICT COURT

DEFINITION: _____

_____

_____

EXAMPLE: _____

_____

_____

FEDERAL APPEALS COURT

DEFINITION: _____

_____

_____

EXAMPLE: _____

_____

_____

U.S SUPREME COURT

DEFINITION: _____

_____

_____

EXAMPLE: _____

_____

_____

QUESTIONS: WHAT IS THE HIGHEST COURT IN NY?

_____

IN NEW JERSEY?

_____

IN THE UNITED STATES?

_____

WHY ARE THEY NOT THE SAME?

_____

ASSIGNMENT WEEK #4

LITIGATION

DEFINITION: _____

_____

_____

EXAMPLE: _____

_____

_____

VENUE

DEFINITION: _____

_____

_____

EXAMPLE: _____

_____

_____

STANDING TO SUE

DEFINITION: _____

_____

_____

EXAMPLE: _____

_____

_____

VALID LEGAL CONTROVERSY

DEFINITION: _____

_____

_____

EXAMPLE: _____

_____

_____

STATUTE OF LIMITATIONS

DEFINITION: _____

_____

_____

EXAMPLE: _____

_____

_____

DAMAGES

DEFINITION: _____

_____

_____

EXAMPLE: _____

_____

_____

ALTERNATIVE DISPUTE RESOLUTION

DEFINITION: _____

_____

_____

EXAMPLE: _____

_____

_____

SUMMONS

DEFINITION: _____

_____

_____

EXAMPLE: _____

_____

_____

ANSWER

DEFINITION: _____

_____

_____

EXAMPLE: _____

_____

_____

COMPLAINT

DEFINITION: _____

_____

_____

EXAMPLE: _____

_____

_____

CLASS ACTION LAWSUIT

DEFINITION: _____

_____

_____

EXAMPLE: _____

_____

CAN A CLASS ACTION LAWSUIT BE BENEFICIAL?

_____

Norgart v Upjohn Company

Supreme Court of California (1999)

FACTS:

Kristi Bogart McBride was married and suffered from manic-depression (now called bi-polar disorder) and due to this disease, attempted suicide by overdosing on drugs. In addition, her husband had physically abused Kristi. The doctor prescribed Halcion, a sedative-hypnotic drug, and Darvocet, a narcotic. In 1985, Kristi, severely depressed, committed suicide by overdosing on a combination of both drugs. Two bottles of both drugs were found near her bed when her body was found. The combination of these two drugs when combined had an adverse effect on Kristi, making her condition worse. In 1986, her parents suspected that the drugs/abuse were the cause of death but did not take any legal action at that time. In 1991, Kristi's parents filed a wrongful death lawsuit against the Upjohn Company, for failure to warn of the dangers of taking Darvocet. The Upjohn Company took this case to the Supreme Court of California, alleging that the Statute of Limitations for the parents to file this case had run out and that the case should have been filed within one year from the time of Kristi's death as mandated by law.

ISSUE:

Are the parents barred (stopped) by the one-year statute of limitations for wrongful death?

DECISION:

Yes

OPINION:

The Supreme Court held that the one-year statute of limitations had run out and that the parents were barred from bringing the case against Upjohn. Legally, the Nogarts were required to bring this case forward within one year of Kristi's death. There is no triable issue of fact for the Court to consider, and therefore dismiss the case in favor of Upjohn.

QUESTIONS TO ANSWER:

Do you agree with the decision of the Supreme Court? _____

Why have a statute of limitations? _____

What is the purpose?_____

Why do you think there is a one-year statute of limitations on wrongful death?_____

_____

Do you think that Kristi's doctor should also be held accountable for prescribing both drugs?_____

Halcion is used to treat mood disorders and insomnia

Darvocet, which is a synthetic opioid, used for pain was taken off the market by the FDA in 2010

ASSIGNMENT FOR WEEKS # 5 & # 6

CONTRACT

DEFINITION: _____

_____

_____

EXAMPLE: _____

_____

_____

OFFEROR

DEFINITION: _____

_____

_____

EXAMPLE: _____

_____

_____

OFFEREE

DEFINITION: _____

_____

_____

EXAMPLE: _____

_____

_____

COMMON LAW OF CONTRACTS

DEFINITION: _____

_____

_____

EXAMPLE: _____

_____

_____

UNIFORM COMMERCIAL CODE

DEFINITION: _____

_____

_____

EXAMPLE: _____

_____

_____

RESTATEMENT OF CONTRACTS

DEFINITION: _____

_____

_____

EXAMPLE: _____

_____

_____

EXPRESS CONTRACT

DEFINITION: _____

_____

_____

EXAMPLE: _____

_____

_____

UNILATERAL CONTRACT

DEFINITION: _____

_____

_____

EXAMPLE: _____

_____

_____

BILATERAL CONTRACT

DEFINITION: _____

_____

_____

EXAMPLE: _____

_____

_____

EXECUTORY CONTRACT

DEFINITION: _____

_____

_____

EXAMPLE: _____

_____

_____

EXECUTED CONTRACT

DEFINITION: _____

_____

_____

EXAMPLE: _____

_____

_____

VOIDABLE CONTRACT

DEFINITION: _____

_____

EXAMPLE: _____

_____

_____

VOID CONTRACT

DEFINITION: _____

_____

_____

EXAMPLE: _____

_____

_____

IMPLIED CONTRACT

DEFINITION: _____

_____

_____

EXAMPLE: _____

_____

_____

IMPLIED-IN-LAW CONTRACT

DEFINITION: _____

_____

_____

EXAMPLE: _____

_____

_____

IMPLIED-IN-FACT CONTRACT

DEFINITION: _____

_____

_____

EXAMPLE: _____

_____

_____

EQUITY

DEFINITION: _____

_____

_____

EXAMPLE: _____

_____

_____

OBJECTIVE THEORY OF CONTRACTS

DEFINITION: _____

_____

_____

EXAMPLE: _____

_____

_____

City of Everett, Washington v Mitchell

Supreme Court of Washington 1981

FACTS:

Al and Rosemary Mitchell were the owners of a small secondhand store and attended many auctions to purchase merchandise to sell. In 1978, the Mitchells attended Alexander's Auction, which they frequently went to for merchandise. At the auction, there was a sale on a safe that was part of the Sumstad Estate. An estate sale is a means of liquidating items that were left by death. The Mitchell's bid and paid $50 for the safe and were told that the inside of the safe was locked and that there was no key to unlock the safe. The Mitchell's took the safe to a locksmith several days after the purchase to have the locked compartment opened. The locksmith opened the safe, found $32,207 in cash, and called the City of Everett's police department to report the found money. Upon notice, the City of Everett started a case against the Mitchells to recover the money found in the safe. The claim was that they were legally entitled to the money from the Sumstad Estate and that they did not own the "inside" of the safe, but only the "outside."

ISSUES:

Was a contract formed between the buyer and seller of the safe at the auction?

Do the Mitchell's own both the outside and inside of the safe?

Does the City of Everett have a legal claim upon the money?

DECISIONS:

Yes, Yes, No

OPINION:

The State Supreme Court held that under the "Objective Theory of Contracts," a valid sale existed between the seller and the buyer. The auction stated that all sales were "final" and the Mitchell's purchased the safe in good faith and therefore were legally entitled to the money found in the safe.

QUESTIONS TO ANSWER:

Do you agree with the decision of the Court? _____

Do you think the sale is valid? _____

Would the Mitchell's have agreed to purchase only the outside of the safe?

_____

What is the "Objective Theory of Contracts?"

_____

How is it used?

_____

What does a "reasonable person" mean?

_____

Is it the same as an "average person?"_____

Did the locksmith act ethically under the circumstances? _____

What could the auctioneer have said to prevent this?

_____

_____

NOTES AND ASSIGNMENTS

NOTES AND ASSIGNMENTS

TERMS OF A K – WHAT DO YOU NEED TO INCLUDE IN A K?

WHAT ARE THE REQUIREMENTS FOR A VALID K?

OFFER

DEFINITION: _____

_____

_____

EXAMPLE: _____

_____

_____

COUNTEROFFER

DEFINITION: _____

_____

_____

EXAMPLE: _____

_____

_____

EVOCATION

DEFINITION: _____

_____

_____

EXAMPLE: _____

_____

_____

REWARD

DEFINITION: _____

_____

EXAMPLE: _____

_____

_____

AUCTIONS

DEFINITION: _____

_____

_____

EXAMPLE: _____

_____

_____

BIDS IN AUCTIONS

DEFINITION: _____

_____

_____

EXAMPLE: _____

_____

_____

AUCTIONS WITH RESERVE

DEFINITION: _____

_____

_____

EXAMPLE: _____

_____

_____

AUCTIONS WITHOUT RESERVE

DEFINITION: _____

_____

_____

EXAMPLE: _____

_____

_____

ACCEPTANCE

DEFINITION: _____

_____

_____

EXAMPLE: _____

_____

_____

MANIFESTATION OF ASSENT

DEFINITION: _____

_____

_____

EXAMPLE: _____

_____

_____

MAILBOX RULE

DEFINITION: _____

_____

_____

EXAMPLE: _____

_____

MIRROR IMAGE RULE

DEFINITION: _____

_____

_____

EXAMPLE: _____

_____

_____

SILENCE AS ACCEPTANCE

DEFINITION: _____

_____

_____

EXAMPLE: _____

_____

_____

CONSIDERATION

DEFINITION: _____

_____

_____

EXAMPLE: _____

_____

_____

TANGIBLE CONSIDERATION

DEFINITION: _____

_____

_____

EXAMPLE: _____

_____

INTANGIBLE CONSIDERATION

DEFINITION: _____

EXAMPLE: _____

_____

_____

PROMISES

DEFINITION: _____

_____

_____

EXAMPLE: _____

_____

_____

PROMISSORY ESTOPPEL

DEFINITION: _____

_____

_____

EXAMPLE: _____

_____

_____

Alden v Presley

Supreme Court of Tennessee 1982

FACTS:

Elvis Presley was a well-known singer and had acquired substantial wealth over his career. Elvis died on August 16th, 1977, of an apparent heart attack and was found in his bathroom at Graceland. Elvis was engaged to Ginger Alden at the time of his death and was known to be very generous. This included Ginger Alden and her family by paying for landscaping, installing swimming pools, and other generous gifts. Jo Laverne Alden was the mother of Ginger and sought to divorce her husband. Jo Laverne Alden had an unpaid mortgage of $39,587 from the divorce, which Elvis promised to pay. Elvis died and left the mortgage unpaid, and the legal representation of the Presley Estate refused to pay the mortgage.

Jo Laverne Alden brought a legal action against the estate to enforce and recover the money that had been promised by Elvis.

ISSUES:

Was the promise made by Elvis to pay the mortgage enforceable?

Was there any consideration?

Is the promise a "gift?"

DECISIONS:

No, No, Yes

OPINION:

The Supreme Court held that the promise was not enforceable against the estate. In law, promises are not enforceable unless there is an exchange of consideration. The promise was considered executory and therefore unenforceable since Elvis had not completed it, and his estate was not responsible for doing so. The Court also found that the promise was considered a "gift" under law.

QUESTIONS TO ANSWER:

Do you agree with the decision of the Court? _____

Why are promises not enforceable?

_____

What is meant by "consideration?"

_____

Did the estate act ethically? _____

Could Mrs. Alden have done anything to enforce the promise?

_____

_____

Why do you think this case went to the Supreme Court of Tennessee?

_____

Who do you think was the legal representative of the estate?

_____

Does the estate still make money today and who would be entitled to it?

_____

NOTES AND ASSIGNMENTS

ASSIGNMENT WEEK # 9

CAPACITY

DEFINITION: _____

_____

_____

EXAMPLE: _____

_____

_____

MINOR

DEFINITION: _____

_____

_____

EXAMPLE: _____

_____

_____

INFANCY DOCTRINE

DEFINITION: _____

_____

_____

EXAMPLE: _____

_____

_____

NECESSITIES/NECESSARIES OF LIFE FOR THE MINOR

DEFINITION: _____

_____

_____

EXAMPLE: _____

_____

_____

DISAFFIRMANCE

DEFINITION: _____

_____

_____

EXAMPLE: _____

_____

_____

RATIFICATION

DEFINITION: _____

_____

_____

EXAMPLE: _____

_____

_____

PARENTAL DUTY

DEFINITION: _____

_____

_____

EXAMPLE: _____

_____

_____

EMANCIPATION

DEFINITION: _____

_____

_____

EXAMPLE: _____

_____

_____

RESTITUTION

DEFINITION: _____

_____

_____

EXAMPLE: _____

_____

_____

RESTORATION

DEFINITION: _____

_____

_____

EXAMPLE: _____

_____

_____

INCOMPETENT (INSANE)

DEFINITION: _____

_____

_____

EXAMPLE: _____

_____

_____

ADJUDGED/ADJUDICATED INCOMPETENT

DEFINITION: _____

_____

EXAMPLE: _____

_____

_____

INTOXICATION

DEFINITION: _____

_____

_____

EXAMPLE: _____

_____

_____

ILLEGALITY

DEFINITION: _____

_____

_____

EXAMPLE: _____

_____

_____

USURY

DEFINITION: _____

_____

_____

EXAMPLE: _____

_____

GAMBLING

DEFINITION: _____

_____

EXAMPLE: _____

_____

_____

BLUE/SABBATH LAWS

DEFINITION: _____

_____

_____

EXAMPLE: _____

_____

_____

K'S CONTRARY TO PUBLIC POLICY

DEFINITION: _____

_____

_____

EXAMPLE: _____

_____

_____

_____

UNCONSCIONABLE K'S

DEFINITION: _____

_____

_____

EXAMPLE: _____

_____

_____

_____

Jones v Free Flight Sport Aviation, Inc.

Supreme Court of Colorado 1981

FACTS:

William Michael Jones was a 17-year-old minor when in signed a contract in 1973 with Free Flight Sport Aviation. The contract was for his recreational use of their skydiving facilities for parachute jumping. The contract contained an exculpatory clause and a covenant not to sue. Jones turned 18 years old and reached the age of majority. He continued to use the facilities at Free Flight for ten months after turning 18 years old. Jones was on a skydiving mission when the airplane crashed shortly after take-off from the airport. Free Flight provided the airplane that crashed. Jones suffered severe personal injuries in the crash. Jones then sued the aviation company claiming that they were negligent and responsible for his injuries.

ISSUES:

Did Jones ratify the contract?

Is the exculpatory clause valid?

Is the covenant not to sue valid?

Could Jones still be considered a minor?

DECISIONS:

Yes, Yes, Yes, No

OPINION:

The Supreme Court held that Free Flight Sport Aviation was not liable for the injuries sustained by Jones. A minor may disaffirm a contract during their minority or within a reasonable time after attaining the age of majority. Here, Jones had ratified the contract. In addition, the Court said that Jones had accepted the risks involved when he used Free Flight's facilities and that he lacked standing to sue based on the conditions of the contract.

QUESTIONS TO ANSWER:

Do you agree with the decision of the court? _____

Should Jones be allowed to disaffirm the contract? _____

Why are the exculpatory clauses and covenants not to sue valid here?

_____

Should minors be allowed to sign contracts? _____

What can a company do to prevent minors from disaffirming a contract?

_____

Courts want to protect minors. Why? _____

ASSIGNMENT WEEK # 10

DEFENSES TO ENFORCING A K

DEFINITION: _____

_____

_____

EXAMPLE: _____

_____

_____

GENUINENESS OF ASSENT

DEFINITION: _____

_____

_____

EXAMPLE: _____

_____

_____

MEETING OF MINDS

DEFINITION: _____

_____

_____

EXAMPLE: _____

_____

_____

UNILATERAL MISTAKE

DEFINITION: _____

_____

_____

EXAMPLE: _____

_____

_____

MUTUAL MISTAKE

DEFINITION: _____

_____

_____

EXAMPLE: _____

_____

_____

FRAUD

DEFINITION: _____

_____

_____

EXAMPLE: _____

_____

_____

UNDUE INFLUENCE

DEFINITION: _____

_____

_____

EXAMPLE: _____

_____

_____

DURESS

DEFINITION: _____

_____

_____

EXAMPLE: _____

_____

_____

STATUTE OF FRAUDS

DEFINITION: _____

_____

_____

EXAMPLE: _____

_____

_____

PAROL (WORD) EVIDENCE RULE

DEFINITION: _____

_____

_____

EXAMPLE: _____

_____

_____

Wells Fargo Credit Corp. v Martin

Court of Appeals Florida 1992

FACTS:

Mr. and Mrs. Clevenger owned a home that went into foreclosure. The value of the home was listed as $207,141 and was to be sold at an auction. Foreclosure sales are ways many people seek to buy properties, cars, jewelry, etc. Wells Fargo sent a paralegal as their representative to the auction because the paralegal had been to more than 1,000 comparable sales. Wells Fargo gave the paralegal handwritten instructions to bid $115,000 for the property. The paralegal misread the instructions because the "1" was remarkably close to the "$" sign and opened the bidding at the auction for $15,000 instead of $115,000! Harley Martin also attended the auction after his current home had been severely damaged due to a fire. He heard the first bid and raised it to $20,000. There were no other bids after the auctioneer gave ample time for someone else to bid on the property. The auctioneer then said, "going once, twice, sold to Harley Martin for $20,000." The paralegal immediately jumped up and screamed, "I am sorry, I made a mistake!" Mr. Martin then made sure that the certificate of ownership was issued to him despite the objections of the paralegal. Wells Fargo then sought to overturn the sale based on the unilateral mistake of the paralegal.

ISSUES:

Is a unilateral mistake valid to overturn the sale?

Should Mr. Martin retain ownership of the property?

Was the auction sale final under the circumstances?

DECISIONS:

No, Yes, Yes

OPINION:

The Appellate Court held that the sale was final when the auctioneer said, "sold to Harley Martin!" A unilateral mistake is generally not a valid defense to overturn the contract. In addition, the circumstances surrounding the sale were in favor of Mr. Martin, not Wells Fargo. The Court does agree the sale was grossly underpaid for the property, but this fact does not warrant the sale to be declared invalid. The mistake of the paralegal is on Wells Fargo.

QUESTIONS TO ANSWER:

Do you agree with the decision of the Court? _____

Did Wells Fargo act ethically in trying to overturn the sale? _____

Does the "reasonable person standard apply here? How?

_____

_____

Do these types of mistakes often happen in business?

_____

Is a unilateral mistake a valid defense here?

_____

_____

How can these mistakes be avoided?

_____

_____

_____

Konic International Corp. v Spokane Computer Services, Inc.

Court of Appeals of Idaho 1985

FACTS:

David Young was an employee of Spokane Computer Services. The company instructed him to do research for the purchase of a computer power surge, which is a device that protects computers from damaging electrical currents. Mr. Young investigated several possibilities that were in the price range of $50 to $200. However, none of them perfectly suited the needs of the company. Mr. Young contacted Konic International by telephone and was referred to a salesclerk who managed these sales. The salesperson described a device that was appropriate for Spokane and when asked the price by Mr. Young quoted "fifty-six twenty." Mr. Young ordered the unit by telephone, and it was later shipped and installed. Two weeks later an error was discovered when the bill arrived and claimed the amount due was $5,620! Mr. Young claimed he thought the quoted price was $56.20! Konic refused to take back the power surge and sued Spokane for the unpaid balance.

ISSUES:

Was there a mutual mistake?

Should the contract be rescinded?

Was the expressed price ambiguous?

DECISIONS:

Yes, Yes, Yes

OPINION:

The Appellate Court held that a mutual mistake had occurred and that the contract should be rescinded. The Court further said that there was no "meeting of minds" between the parties. The expressed price was ambiguous under the circumstances and each party had concluded a different meaning to the contract, thus making a mutual mistake a valid defense. Price is considered an integral part of a contract and is a material term. Here, the agreement between the parties was not genuine and thus, the contract should be rescinded in favor of Spokane. When both parties are mistaken as to the essential terms of a contract, neither party should be held responsible. In addition, there was a failure of communication between the parties as well under the circumstances.

QUESTIONS TO ANSWER:

Do you agree with the decision of the court? _____

Are mutual mistakes valid defenses?

_____

_____

Does the "reasonable person standard" apply here? _____

What is meant by "meeting of the minds?" _____

Wilson v Western National Life Insurance Co.

Court of Appeals of California 1991

FACTS:

Daniel and Doris Wilson were married and in 1985, Daniel fainted from a narcotics overdose and was rushed to the hospital, unconscious. Daniel recovered and the doctor at the hospital noted that Daniel suffered from a heroin overdose and that he had multiple puncture sites on his arms from use. An insurance agent from Western met with the Wilsons in their home for the purpose of applying for life insurance. The representative asked the Wilsons the following questions and recorded them on the written application form: "In the past 10 years, have you been treated for alcoholism or drug addition," and in the past 5 years, have you been treated or examined by any physician?" The Wilsons answered "no" to both questions, signed the application, and paid the premium for the first month. The $50,000 life insurance policy took effect immediately. Daniel died from a drug overdose two days after signing the policy! Doris Wilson sought to claim the $50,000 death benefit but Western rejected the claim for failing to disclose the drug incident and hospitalization by the Wilsons.

ISSUES:

Should the contract be rescinded?

Did the Wilsons commit fraud?

Did the Wilsons act ethically?

DECISIONS:

Yes, Yes, No

OPINION:

The Appellate Court held that there was a concealment of fact by the Wilsons or a misrepresentation and thus, the contract should be rescinded. This concealment was of a material fact and the life insurance company would not have issued the policy had the information been known to them. Western had relied on the Wilsons and had would be subsequently injured if the company had to pay the $50,000 death benefit. Otherwise, the insurance company would have been liable for the death benefits to be paid to Doris Wilson even though in effect for only two days.

QUESTIONS TO ANSWER:

Do you agree with the decision of the court? _____

Is fraud a valid defense? _____

Did the Wilsons act ethically? _____

Should the Insurance Company have relied on the words of the Wilsons? _____

How do Insurance Companies prevent this from happening today?

_____

NOTES AND ASSIGNMENTS

ASSIGNMENT WEEK # 11

PRIVITY OF K

DEFINITION: _____

_____

_____

EXAMPLE: _____

_____

_____

3RD PARTY RIGHTS IN K'S

DEFINITION: _____

_____

_____

EXAMPLE: _____

_____

_____

ASSIGNMENT

DEFINITION: _____

_____

_____

EXAMPLE: _____

_____

_____

DELEGATION

DEFINITION: _____

_____

_____

EXAMPLE: _____

_____

_____

INTENDED BENEFICIARY

DEFINITION: _____

_____

_____

EXAMPLE: _____

_____

_____

DONEE BENEFICIARY

DEFINITION: _____

_____

_____

EXAMPLE: _____

_____

_____

CREDITOR BENEFICIARY

DEFINITION: _____

_____

_____

EXAMPLE: _____

_____

_____

INCIDENTAL BENEFICIARY

DEFINITION: _____

_____

_____

EXAMPLE: _____

_____

_____

MUTUAL RESCISSION

DEFINITION: _____

_____

_____

EXAMPLE: _____

_____

_____

DISCHARGE OF PERFORMANCE

DEFINITION: _____

_____

_____

EXAMPLE: _____

_____

_____

IMPOSSIBILIITY OF PERFORMANCE

DEFINITION: _____

_____

_____

EXAMPLE: _____

_____

_____

_____

_____

Parker v Arthur Murray Dance Studios, Inc.

Appellate Court of Illinois 1973

FACTS:

In 1959, Ryland Parker was a 37-year-old college educated bachelor. He lived alone in a one-room attic apartment and had received and redeemed a certificate to for three free dance lessons from Arthur Murray dance studios. The instructor told him during the free lessons that he had "exceptional potential to be a fine and accomplished dancer!" Parker thereupon signed a contract for more lessons. He continued his lessons and was praised by his instructors despite his lack of progress. He made extensions for his contract and each extension contained in bold type the following words: "NONCANCELABLE CONTRACT AND I UNDERSTAND THAT NO REFUNDS WILL BE MADE UNDER THE TERMS OF THIS CONTRACT!" Mr. Parker eventually signed up for 2,734 lessons for which he prepaid $24,812! Mr. Parker was subsequently injured in an automobile accident that rendered him unable to continue his dance lessons. Therefore, he sought to rescind the contract. The studio refused to refund any of his money based on the fact that the terms of the contract were agreed upon and could not be canceled or any of the monies refunded.

ISSUES:

Does the doctrine of impossibility apply here?

Should the contract be rescinded?

DECISIONS:

Yes, Yes

OPINION:

The Appellate Court held that the doctrine of impossibility is recognized as grounds for rescission of a contract. The studio's claim that the clause was specifically entered into and agreed upon by the parties to prevent the doctrine of impossibility from being applied. Furthermore, there is no way Mr. Parker could have anticipated this would or could happen and not to excuse him from the contract would be grossly unfair to him. The duty to perform exists in every contract as agreed but certain circumstances must be considered and here it is clear that this duty is not possible.

QUESTIONS TO ANSWER:

Do you agree with the decision of the court? _____

What other grounds would constitute impossibility of performance?

_____

What is meant by the "duty to perform?" _____

Do contracts still contain these terms today? _____

Why do you think Mr. Parker agreed to these terms of the contract?

_____

ASSIGNMENT FOR WEEK # 12

DAMAGES

DEFINITION: _____

_____

_____

EXAMPLE: _____

_____

_____

BREACH OF K

DEFINITION: _____

_____

_____

EXAMPLE: _____

_____

_____

LEGAL REMEDY

DEFINITION: _____

_____

_____

EXAMPLE: _____

_____

_____

COMPENSATORY DAMAGES

DEFINITION: _____

_____

_____

EXAMPLE: _____

_____

_____

CONSEQUENTIAL DAMAGES

DEFINITION: _____

_____

_____

EXAMPLE: _____

_____

_____

PUNITIVE DAMAGES

DEFINITION: _____

_____

_____

EXAMPLE: _____

_____

_____

LIQUIDATED DAMAGES

DEFINITION: _____

_____

_____

EXAMPLE: _____

_____

_____

NOMINAL DAMAGES

DEFINITION: _____

_____

_____

EXAMPLE: _____

_____

_____

EQUITABLE REMEDY

DEFINITION: _____

_____

_____

EXAMPLE: _____

_____

_____

INJUNCTION

DEFINITION: _____

_____

_____

EXAMPLE: _____

_____

_____

SPECIFIC PERFORMANCE

DEFINITION: _____

_____

_____

EXAMPLE: _____

_____

_____

REFORMATION

DEFINITION: _____

_____

EXAMPLE: _____

_____

_____

MITIGATION

DEFINITION: _____

_____

_____

EXAMPLE: _____

_____

_____

Parker v Twentieth Century-Fox Film Corp.

Supreme Court of California 1970

FACTS:

Shirley MacLaine Parker was a well-known actor as well as a dancer. Twentieth Century-Fox was a major film production studio and offered Ms. Parker an employment contract. The contract required Ms. Parker to play the leading role in a musical called "Bloomer Girl" to be filmed in Los Angeles. The contract was for 14 weeks, with a salary of $53,571.42 for a total upon completion of $750,000. The starting date was May 1966. In April 1966, Fox sent Ms. Parker a letter stating that the movie would not be filmed but offered her the leading role in another film called "Big Country," which was a dramatic western to be filmed in Australia. The compensation and terms were the same and Fox gave Ms. Parker one week to accept. Ms. Parker did not accept and the offer expired. Fox refused to pay her, and Ms. Parker sued for compensation.

ISSUES:

Is Parker due the $750,000 under the contract?

Does Parker have to accept the new role?

Were the roles similar or comparable?

Does Parker have a duty to mitigate?

Is it reasonable for Parker to mitigate under the circumstances?

DECISIONS:

Yes, No, No, Yes, No

OPINION:

The Supreme Court held that the employer must show that the other offer was comparable, or substantially similar to the first one. It was clear here that the two roles are not similar, and that Ms. Parker's talents would not be put to use in the new film. Ms. Parker was known and hired as an actress/dancer and not as a dramatic actor and therefore, could refuse the new role under the circumstances. The second offer was both different and inferior to the original one, thus releasing Ms. Parker of her duty to perform or accept the second offer.

QUESTIONS TO ANSWER:

Do you agree with the decision of the court?

_____

What was Twentieth Century-Fox trying to do here?

_____

_____

Under what circumstances would Ms. Parker have to consider accepting the new role?

_____

_____

How are damages measured here?

_____

_____

What type(s) of damages are applicable?

_____

_____

Why is mitigation imposed upon the innocent (non-breaching) party?

_____

_____

How are these situations avoided today?

_____

_____

NOTES AND ASSIGNMENTS

ASSIGNMENT FOR WEEK # 13

UNIFORM COMMERCIAL CODE ARTICLE 2 (SALES)

DEFINITION: _____

_____

_____

EXAMPLE: _____

_____

_____

GOODS

DEFINITION: _____

_____

_____

EXAMPLE: _____

_____

_____

MERCHANT

DEFINITION: _____

_____

_____

EXAMPLE: _____

_____

_____

SALE

DEFINITION: _____

_____

_____

EXAMPLE: _____

_____

_____

MIXED SALE

DEFINITION: _____

_____

_____

EXAMPLE: _____

_____

_____

TITLE

DEFINITION: _____

_____

_____

EXAMPLE: _____

_____

_____

RISK OF LOSS

DEFINITION: _____

_____

_____

EXAMPLE: _____

_____

_____

FIRM OFFER RULE

DEFINITION: _____

_____

_____

EXAMPLE: _____

_____

_____

NEGLIGENCE

DEFINITION: _____

_____

_____

EXAMPLE: _____

_____

_____

WARRANTY

DEFINITION: _____

_____

_____

EXAMPLE: _____

_____

_____

BREACH OF WARRANTY

DEFINITION: _____

_____

_____

EXAMPLE: _____

_____

_____

EXPRESS WARRANTY

DEFINITION: _____

_____

EXAMPLE: _____

_____

_____

IMPLIED WARRANTY

DEFINITION: _____

_____

_____

EXAMPLE: _____

_____

_____

FOREIGN SUBSTANCE TEST & CONSUMER EXPECTATION TEST – (RELATES TO FOOD)

DEFINITION: _____

_____

_____

EXAMPLE: _____

_____

_____

STRICT PRODUCT LIABILITY

DEFINITION: _____

_____

_____

EXAMPLE: _____

_____

_____

DISCLAIMERS

DEFINITION: _____

Hector v Cedars-Sinai Medical Center

Appellate Court of California 1986

FACTS:

Ms. Frances Hector went to Cedars-Sinai hospital in Los Angeles. She needed a surgical operation on her heart, which required the installation of a pacemaker. A pacemaker are electrical wires connected to the heart to help it pump efficiently. Ms. Hector's pacemaker was made by American Technology, Inc., and was installed by her physician at the hospital. After installation, the pacemaker was defective and caused severe injury and harm to Ms. Hector. She sued the hospital under Article 2 of the Uniform Commercial Code (UCC) claiming the hospital was responsible for her injuries. The purpose of the UCC is to make it easier for the public to sue manufacturers in commerce. However, the doctor had specifically ordered the type of pacemaker to be installed.

ISSUES:

Is the hospital liable for defects in medical products?

Can Ms. Hector sue the hospital under the UCC?

Can Ms. Hector sue American Technology under the UCC?

Can Ms. Hector sue the hospital under common law?

Do services fall under the UCC?

DECISIONS:

No, No, Yes, Maybe, No

OPINION:

The Appellate court held that hospitals are not usually engaged in the business of selling products but is more of a provider of services. The hospital is liable for the services provided and normally not subject to liability if the product is defective. The hospital provided pre- and post-operative care, nursing care, an operating room, and technicians. There was no evidence of any misdoings in any of these procedures. Thus, this removes the hospital from liability under the UCC.

QUESTIONS TO ANSWER:

Do you agree with the decision of the court? _____

Was the hospital liable here? _____

What common law theory could Ms. Hector sue the hospital?

_____

Why did Ms. Hector sue the hospital and not the manufacturer of the pacemaker?

_____

What is a "mixed sale" under the UCC and what does that mean for Ms. Hector?

_____

Daughtrey v Ashe

Supreme Court of Virginia 1992

FACTS:

Mr. W.H. Daughtrey went to see a jeweler, Mr. Sidney Ashe, in 1985. Mr. Daughtrey consulted with the jeweler about purchasing a diamond bracelet for his wife as a present for Christmas. Mr. Daughtrey selected a diamond bracelet valued at $15,000. Mr. Ashe gave him an appraisal form with the following specifications: "The diamonds were H color and v.v.s. quality." (Diamonds are valued by their color with H being colorless and highly valued, and v.v.s. is one of the highest ratings employed by jewelers). The bracelet and form were put in a decorative box, which was given to Mrs. Daughtrey at Christmas. In 1987, Mrs. Daughtrey took the bracelet to another jeweler who determined that the diamonds did not meet the standards specified, and in fact, were of much lower quality. Mr. Daughtrey returned the bracelet to Mr. Ashe insisting he either replace the diamonds or pay the difference in value. Mr. Ashe refused both options claiming that the appraisal form was for insurance purposes only and did not constitute any warranty.

ISSUES:

Was a warranty formed between the seller and the buyer?

Did the description of the diamonds create a "benefit of bargain" in the contract?

Were the statements made by Ashe opinions?

Were the statements made by Ashe facts?

DECISIONS:

Yes, Yes, No, Yes

OPINION:

The Supreme Court held that an express warranty was created between the buyer and the seller. Any description of goods that form the benefit of bargain in a contract requires that the goods conform to the standards. Furthermore, it was not necessary for Ashe to use the words "warrant or guarantee" to create a warranty and Daughtrey had relied to his detriment on the statements made to him by Ashe.

QUESTIONS TO ANSWER:

Do you agree with the decision of the court? _____

Did Ashe act ethically in refusing to honor the appraisal? _____

Did the statements made by Ashe have to be in writing? Oral? Both?

_____

_____

How would the "reasonable person standard" apply here?

_____

Goodman v Wendy's Foods, Inc.

Supreme Court of North Carolina 1992

FACTS:

In 1983, Mr. Goodman went to a Wendy's restaurant, where he purchased a hamburger with "everything" on it. Mr. Goodman ate about half of the hamburger when he bit a hard substance. He bit a steak bone that was 1.5 inches long and ¼ inch wide. This caused him to break three of his teeth, which required him to have dental treatment, surgery, root canal work, and crowns to replace the broken teeth. This resulted in substantial damage from the costs of all the dental work. He sued Wendy's for breach of an implied warranty of fitness for human consumption. Wendy's claimed that the foreign substance test applied, and that they were protected from liability. In addition, a steak bone was not foreign to hamburgers, which are made from steak (cows) and that it is "natural" not "foreign." In addition, Wendy's could not have discovered the steak bone in the hamburger.

ISSUES:

Is Wendy's liable for the damage sustained by Mr. Goodman?

Does the foreign substance test apply?

Does the consumer expectation test apply?

Are steak bones natural to hamburgers?

DECISIONS:

Yes, No, Yes, No

OPINION:

The Supreme Court held that the consumer expectation test applied here, not the foreign substance test. Furthermore, a restaurant makes an implied warranty to its consumers that the food will be fit for consumption. This places the onus on manufacturers of food to make sure that the products they distribute are safe for consumption. Consumers rely on restaurants where the foods served have met the standards. Therefore, Wendy's is liable for the damage sustained by Goodman.

QUESTIONS TO ANSWER:

Do you agree with the decision of the court? _____

Did Wendy's act ethically in denying responsibility? _____

Why have a narrower test for implied warranties for food?

_____

What would be considered "natural" to be found in hamburgers? _____

Why does "food" fall under the UCC? _____

Can consumers reasonably expect all foods to be safe?

_____

Dolinski v Coca-Cola Bottling Co.

Supreme Court of Nevada 1967

FACTS:

Mr. Leo Dolinski worked at Sea and Ski Plant Company. There was a vending machine where Mr. Dolinski purchased a bottle of "Squirt," which was a lemon-lime soft drink. He opened the bottle and drank about 50% of the soft drink when he became suddenly ill. The soda was examined and found to contain the following: "decomposed mouse, mouse hair, and mouse feces." Mr. Dolinski sought medical treatment and was given medicine to combat his nausea. He suffered physical and emotional distress from the incident and now possessed an aversion to all soft drinks. "Squirt" was manufactured and distributed by the Coca-Cola Company. Mr. Dolinski sued the company on the doctrine of strict product liability. This doctrine had not yet been recognized by the state of Nevada. Mr. Dolinski was asking for compensatory damages due to his extreme emotional and physical injuries.

ISSUES:

Should Nevada adopt the doctrine of strict product liability?

Should this doctrine be applied to soft drinks?

Was Coca-Cola ethical in denying liability?

DECISIONS:

Yes, Yes, No

OPINION:

The Supreme Court of Nevada will adopt the doctrine of strict product liability. In addition, the doctrine does apply to the case at hand. Furthermore, "Public policy demands that one who places upon the market a bottled beverage in a condition dangerous for use must be held strictly liable to the ultimate user for injuries from such use, although the seller has exercised all reasonable care." Here, there was a defect in the manufacturing and the court awards Mr. Dolinski $2,500 in compensatory damages for the injuries sustained. All involved in this product are to be held accountable for any defective products put into the marketplace for purchase by the consumer.

QUESTIONS TO ANSWER:

Do you agree with the decision of the court? _____

Did Coca-Cola act ethically? _____

Should strict product liability apply to foods and soft drinks as well? _____

What are the benefits to the consumer regarding this doctrine?

_____

What must the manufacturer consider with this doctrine?

_____

Should liability be placed only on those at fault, or all involved?

_____

Nowak v Faberge USA, Inc.

Court of Appeals of Pennsylvania 1994

FACTS:

Faberge manufactures "Aqua Net," an aerosol hair spray sold in a can. The product contains a mixture of butane or propane to propel the aerosol from the nozzle of the can, and alcohol as a solvent to form a solution, which is hair spray. These products went mixed are extremely flammable and Faberge posts a warning on the back of all cans sold stating the following: "Do not puncture and do not use near an open flame." This warning is clearly visible on the can. Ms. Alison Nowak, a 14-year-old, purchased a new can of hair spray and upon use, the spray valve did not work properly. She then proceeded to puncture the hair spray using a can opener, thinking she could pour the contents into an empty aerosol container, and then use it. She was standing in the kitchen near an oven, with an open gas flame when she punctured the can. Upon puncture, a cloud of hair spray rushed out from the can near the pilot of the stove, which ignited into a ball of flame. She suffered 20% permanent burns over her body, resulting in disfigurement as well. She sued Faberge claiming that the company failed to properly warn of the dangers of flammability.

ISSUES:

Did Faberge adequately warn of the dangers?

Should the doctrine of strict product liability apply here?

DECISIONS:

No, Yes

OPINION:

The Appellate Court held that any manufacturer has a duty to adequately warn users of their products of the dangerous propensities. A product is defective if it fails to adequately warn the consumer of the inherent hazards regarding usage. Public policy supports placing the risks on the manufacturer, and thus, Ms. Nowak is awarded $1.5 million in damages for her injuries, which are permanent and severe from the use of the product.

QUESTIONS TO ANSWER:

Do you agree with the decision of the court? _____

Did Faberge act ethically here? _____

Was the warning clear to the consumer? Why or why not?

_____

_____

_____

Should strict product liability apply to the case at hand?

_____

_____

Should Ms. Nowak be held accountable? Why or why not?

_____

_____

Why do you think the court awarded damages to Ms. Nowak?

_____

_____

What do these decisions impose on any manufacturer of products sold to the public?

_____

_____

If Ms. Nowak sued under negligence or breach of warranty, would it be successful? Why or why not?

_____

_____

NOTES AND ASSIGNMENTS

ASSIGNMENT WEEK # 14

REAL PROPERTY

DEFINITION: _____

_____

_____

EXAMPLE: _____

_____

_____

PERSONAL PROPERTY

DEFINITION: _____

_____

_____

EXAMPLE: _____

_____

_____

INTELLECTUAL PROPERTY

DEFINITION: _____

_____

_____

EXAMPLE: _____

_____

_____

TRADEMARKS

DEFINITION: _____

_____

_____

EXAMPLE: _____

_____

_____

SECONDARY MEANING

DEFINITION: _____

_____

_____

EXAMPLE: _____

_____

_____

COPYRIGHT

DEFINITION: _____

_____

_____

EXAMPLE: _____

_____

_____

PATENTS

DEFINITION: _____

_____

_____

EXAMPLE: _____

_____

_____

DESIGN PATENTS

DEFINITION: _____

_____

_____

EXAMPLE: _____

_____

_____

TRADE DRESS

DEFINITION: _____

_____

_____

EXAMPLE: _____

_____

_____

TRADE SECRETS

DEFINITION: _____

_____

_____

EXAMPLE: _____

_____

_____

FAIR USE DOCTRINE

DEFINITION: _____

_____

_____

EXAMPLE: _____

_____

_____

COUNTERFEIT

DEFINITION: _____

_____

EXAMPLE: _____

_____

_____

KNOCK-OFFS

DEFINITION: _____

_____

_____

EXAMPLE: _____

_____

_____

INFRINGEMENT

DEFINITION: _____

_____

_____

EXAMPLE: _____

_____

_____

UNFAIR COMPETITION

DEFINITION: _____

_____

_____

EXAMPLE: _____

_____

_____

_____

_____

DILUTION

DEFINITION: _____

_____

_____

EXAMPLE: _____

_____

_____

STATE REGISTRATION

DEFINITION: _____

_____

_____

EXAMPLE: _____

_____

_____

FEDERAL REGISTRATION

DEFINITION: _____

_____

_____

EXAMPLE: _____

_____

_____

FALSE ADVERTISING

DEFINITION: _____

_____

_____

EXAMPLE: _____

_____

LANHAM ACT

DEFINITION: _____

_____

_____

EXAMPLE: _____

_____

_____

CEASE & DESIST LETTER

DEFINITION: _____

_____

_____

EXAMPLE: _____

_____

_____

In criminal law, what is a cease & desist order called?

_____

The following cases (see below) all involve the issue(s) of intellectual properties. Please read and think about what the court is trying to decide.

Why are these cases complex?

What concepts, terms, and vocabulary have helped you in preparation of understanding these cases from class?

Qualitex Co. v Jacobson Products Co. U.S. Supreme Court 1995

FACTS:

Qualitex Co., the manufacturer, had for years colored the dry-cleaning press pads it manufactured with a special and distinctive shade of green-gold color. When Jacobson Co., a rival, began to use a similar shade on its own press pads, registered its color as a trademark with the USPTO and filed a trademark infringement case against its rival. The Lanham Act gives a seller or a producer the exclusive right to register a trademark and to prevent competitors from using that trademark. The district court ruled for Jacobson that a trademark could not be obtained for a color alone. Qualitex appealed to the U.S. Supreme Court.

ISSUE:

Can a color alone be registered/protected as a trademark?

DECISION:

Yes

OPINION:

The Court ruled "yes," that a color alone may be registered as a trademark. In addition, there is no objection to the use of a color as a trademark, when that color has attained a secondary meaning linking it with a particular product. The Lanham Act's underlying principles of trademark seem to include color in the realm of what can qualify as a trademark. Thus, a color can sometimes meet the basic requirements without serving any other significant function. This allows competitors to use other colors in a comparable manner.

NOTE: The Lanham Act is the federal law which governs trademarks. Enacted by Congress in 1946, the Act provides for a national system of trademark registration and will protect the owner against the use of similar marks, if such use is likely to result in consumer confusion, or the dilution of a famous mark is likely to occur.

Many things of tenuous tangibility have become trademarks. Ex. Coca-Cola bottle shape, the NBC sounds, thus allowing colors to be the subject of trademarks as well!

Christian Louboutin v Yves Saint Laurent Am. Inc. New York 2012

FACTS:

Christian Louboutin, a fashion designer, sought to stop its competitor Yves Saint Laurent for using the designer's trademark, consisting of a red lacquered outsole on a high fashion woman's shoe. (Red Sole Mark – a red sole on a shoe of a distinct color). The court agreed with YSL that the trademark was likely not enforceable, and Louboutin appealed.

ISSUES:

Is the "red sole mark" entitled to trademark protection? Can a color acquire secondary meaning to qualify for trademark protection?

DECISIONS:

No, Yes

OPINION:

A color cannot be registered as a trademark under the doctrine of "functionality," as clothing is essential and serves a purpose. This meaning makes the "red sole" in a monochromatic setting, unable to be registered as a trademark. However, the "red sole" lacquered outsole that contrasts with the color of the adjoining upper sole, has acquired secondary meaning and is eligible for trademark protection.

Star Athletica L.L.C. v Varsity Brands, Inc. 2017

FACTS:

Varsity Brands, Inc. has more than two hundred copyright registrations for two-dimensional designs – consisting of various lines, chevrons, and colorful shapes – appearing on the surface of cheerleading uniforms that they make and sell. Varsity sued Star Athletica, who also markets cheerleading uniforms, for copyright infringement. Star argued that the copyrights were not valid, as the designs cannot be separated from the uniforms themselves, which makes the designs impossible to copyright. Varsity argued that the designs were separable and non-functional, and therefore the copyrights were valid.

ISSUE:

Are the graphics copyrightable?

DECISION:

Yes

OPINION:

The Court ruled that the designs could be conceptually or physically separated from the uniforms, and therefore are able to be protected under copyright laws. Furthermore, the designs could be "identified separately" and were capable of "existing independently" of the uniforms. The designs here are clearly pictorial, graphical, or sculptural works, which are copyrightable. The copyright for such a work includes the right to reproduce the work and exclude a competitor from doing the same.

Gucci America, Inc. v Guess? Inc. 2012

FACTS:

Gucci claimed that Guess used their trademarks, and one trade dress, in an attempt to "Gucci-fy" their product line. The claims involved the following:

1. The Green-Red-Green Stripe mark (GRG Stripe) used on handbags, luggage and different leather goods; 2. The repeating GG pattern; 3. The Diamond Motif Trade Dress – which is the repeating GG pattern with a pair of inverted G's in each corner rendered in a brown/beige color; 4. The stylized G design mark (Stylized G); and 5; The Script Gucci design mark (Script Gucci).
2. Gucci also seeks a cancellation of Guess's "4G Square repeating logo. Gucci is seeking an injunction against the continued use of its intellectual properties and all monies earned by Guess.

ISSUES:

Should the court issue an injunction to stop Guess from violating Gucci's intellectual properties? Was trade dress an issue: Should Gucci recover all the damages (monies) earned by Guess?

DECISIONS:

Yes, to trademarks; No, to trade dress; No, to damages (monies)

OPINION:

This is a trademark infringement case between two global companies. The Court issues a permanent injunction that would bar (stop) Guess from using the Quarto G Pattern in brown-beige, a Green-Red-Green Stripe (but not stripes with other colors), and certain Square G marks. Guess was allowed to continue using the other marks. On the damages side, out of a $120-million-dollar claim, Gucci was only granted $4.648 million. The Court's decision prompted Gucci to post that they nearly reported $2.7 billion in net revenues in 2011 sales, and that the ruling was merely "a drop in the bucket!"

Lululemon v Calvin Klein 2013

FACTS:

Lululemon is a Vancouver based sportswear giant, instituted a patent infringement lawsuit against Calvin Klein, claiming Calvin Klein infringed on three of its design patents. This was primarily on its design patents for "Astro" yoga pants' signature waistband and design. Lululemon claimed that Calvin Klein's "Performance" brand pants resembled its own "Astro" pants.

ISSUE:

Did Calvin Klein's brand violate Lululemon's design patent?

DECISION:

Unknown

NOTE: Lululemon has withdrawn its lawsuit after the companies agreed to a confidential settlement. Details of the companies' agreement are kept confidential, but this case was considered a game-changer since patent lawsuits are so hard to win in the fashion industry.

Samsung Electronics v Apple Inc. U.S. Supreme Court 2016

FACTS:

Apple sued Samsung Electronics and argued that certain design elements of Samsung's smartphones copied the specific design element in Apple's iPhone. The copy of the design patent only applied to a component of the Samsung smartphone. Apple is seeking damages, all the profits made, from Samsung.

ISSUE:

Should damages be limited to the portion of the design patent copied?

DECISION:

No

OPINION:

The Supreme Court, in a unanimous decision, held that the design patents encompass both the end product, as well as a component of the product. Thus, Samsung would be liable for the total profits earned from using just the component, and not the entire design. Apple was awarded over $1 billion dollars in damages.

Tory Burch v J. Christopher Burch May 2012

FACTS:

Ms. Burch gave Christopher Burch her approval to launch C-Wonder (her brand) to use in his store to sell an assortment of diverse products, including home goods, and non-descript apparel. Ms. Burch claims there was confidential information used by Mr. Burch from his position as Chairman and consultant to Tory Burch, L.L.C. The claim is that Mr. Burch created a "knock-off" and cheaper version of Tory Burch brand items.

ISSUE:

Did Christopher Burch violate the trade secrets of Tory Burch?

DECISION:

Unknown

NOTE: Both parties agreed to a confidential settlement. In addition, Mr. Burch agreed to sell half of his share in Tory Burch, L.L.C.

Details of the settlement are not publicly known. Why?

Alpo Pet Foods v Ralston Purina Co. 1990

FACTS:

The Ralston Purina Company claimed that its dog food was beneficial for dogs with canine hip dysplasia, demonstrating the claims with studies and tests. Alpo Pet Foods brought a claim of false advertising against Purina, stating that the test results could not support the claims made in the advertisements.

ISSUE:

Did Ralston Purina Company falsely advertise its claim?

DECISION:

Yes

OPINION:

The Court held that Purina did make false claims. This is in violation of the Lanham Act, with interstate sales of goods. This false claim would lead to a likelihood of confusion for the consumer, as there was no evidence in support of the claims being made.

NOTE: State and federal laws define the practice of false or misleading advertising as:

The intentional and deliberate act of using deceptive, misleading, or false statements about a product or service, in an advertisement.

Any advertising statements or claims that are deceptive, misleading, or false about a product or service that is being sold to consumers.

See examples below!

Activia yogurt said it had "special bacterial ingredients."

Cheerios can "reduce your cholesterol."

Red Bull said it could "give you wings."

L'Oreal claimed its skincare products were "clinically proven" to "boost genes."

Airborne claimed it could cure the "common cold and flu."

Skechers "shape-ups" sneakers claimed, "Get in shape without setting food in a gym."

The bottom line is:

No business may make false, misleading, or deceptive claims about a product or its services!

Ex. Michael Kors Holdings sued Costco Wholesale Co, accusing the largest U.S. warehouse club retailer of running a "bait-and-switch" false advertising scheme.

Costco claimed handbags for sale at $99.99, while MK bags sell approximately for $298 and $1,195.

Bait and switch is a sales tactic that lures customers in with specific claims about the quality or low prices on items that turn out to be unavailable in order to upsell them on a similar, pricier item.

Is Bait and Switch Legal/Ethical/Illegal/both?

"Bait and switch" is viewed as a crime and is considered a fraudulent sales tactic that is punishable by law as false advertisement under the Lanham Act.

However, it is still commonly used in retail sales business.

NOTES AND ASSIGNMENTS

FASHION BUSINESS LAW

INTELLECTUAL PROPERTIES

SUPPLEMENTAL HANDOUT

PROTECTING

AND

UNDERSTANDING

YOUR

CREATIVE RIGHTS

What is a trademark?

A trademark is a word, phrase, symbol or design, or a combination thereof, that identifies and distinguishes the source of the goods of one party from those of others.

Where can I get basic trademark information?

USPTO.GOV AND Trademark Assistance Center at 1-800-786-9199.

Must I register my trademark?

No. You can establish rights in a mark based on use of the mark in commerce, without registration. However, owning a federal trademark registration on the Principal Register provides several important benefits.

What are the benefits of federal trademark registration?

Owning a federal trademark registration on the Principal Register provides several advantages, including:

- Public notice of your claim of ownership of the mark;
- A legal presumption of your ownership of the mark and your exclusive right to use the mark nationwide on or in connection with the goods/services listed in the registration;
- The ability to bring an action concerning the mark in federal court;
- The use of the U.S. registration as a basis to obtain registration in foreign countries;
- The ability to record the U.S. registration with the U.S. Customs and Border Protection (CBP) to prevent importation of infringing foreign goods;
- The right to use the federal registration symbol ®; and
- Listing in the United States Patent and Trademark Office's online databases.

Do federal regulations govern the use of the designations "TM" or "SM" or the ® symbol?

If you claim rights to use a mark, you may use the "TM" (trademark) or "SM" (service mark) designation to alert the public to your claim of a "common-law" mark. No registration is necessary to use a "TM" or "SM" symbol and you may continue to use these symbols even if the USPTO refuses to register your mark. Those symbols put people on notice that you claim rights in the mark, although common law does not give you all the rights and benefits of federal registration.

You may only use the federal registration symbol "®" after the USPTO actually *registers a mark*, not while an application is pending. Moreover, it may only be used on or in connection with the goods/services listed in the federal trademark registration and while the registration is still alive, (you may not continue to use it if you do not maintain the registration, or it expires). Although there are no specific requirements on where the symbol should be placed relative to the mark, most businesses use the symbol in the upper right corner of the mark. Note: Because several foreign countries use "®" to indicate that a mark is registered in that country, use of the symbol by the holder of a foreign registration may be proper.

Should I have an attorney?

Although not required, most applicants use private trademark attorneys for legal advice regarding use of their trademark, filing an application, and the likelihood of success in the registration process, since not all applications proceed to registration.

Is registration guaranteed and can I get a refund of the money paid?

Registration is not guaranteed and only money paid when not required may be refunded. For information on why registration may be refused,

Should I conduct a search for similar trademarks before filing an application?

It is advisable to conduct a search before filing your application. See TESS TIPS for further information.

Where can I conduct a trademark search for trademarks in pending applications and federal registrations?

You may search the USPTO's Trademark Electronic System (TESS) database free of charge before filing or you may wish to hire an attorney to perform the search and assess the results for you. Alternatively, you can search the database at a Patent and Trademark Resource Center (PTRC). Information about PTRC locations can be found here.

Will the Office conduct a search for me?

The USPTO cannot search your mark for you prior to filing. After filing, the USPTO will conduct a search and will refuse to register your mark if there is another registered or pending mark similar to yours.

Where can I find trademark forms?

You can find USPTO forms through the Trademark Electronic Application System (TEAS). Two forms are available for the initial application: regular TEAS and TEAS Plus. Both forms allow you to pay by credit card, electronic funds transfer, or through an existing United States Patent and Trademark Office (USPTO) deposit account.

If you do not have Internet access, you can access TEAS at any Patent and Trademark Resource Center (PTRC) throughout the United States. Many public libraries also provide Internet access.

We recommend using TEAS, but you may file a paper application. To obtain a printed form, call the Trademark Assistance Center at 1-800-786-9199.

What is the Trademark Electronic Application System (TEAS)?

The system allows you to fill out and file an application form online, paying by credit card, electronic funds transfer, or through an existing USPTO deposit account. TEAS can also be used to file other documents including a response to an examining attorney's Office action, a change of address, an allegation of use, and post registration maintenance documents.

<u>Where do I send mail or make deliveries</u>?

It is recommended you file documents online using TEAS, paper mail may be sent to: Commissioner for Trademarks, P.O. Box 1451, Alexandria, VA 22313-1451. Submissions sent using other delivery services such as Federal Express, United Parcel Service, and DHL is not encouraged, but if used, must be delivered to: Trademark Assistance Center, Madison East, Concourse Level Room C 55, 600 Dulany Street Alexandria, VA 22314.

<u>Who may file an application</u>?

Only the owner of the trademark may file an application for registration. The owner controls the use of the mark and controls the nature and quality of the goods to which it is affixed, or the services for which it is used. The owner may be an individual, corporation, partnership, LLC, or other type of legal entity.

<u>Must I be a U.S. citizen to obtain a federal registration</u>?

No. However, your citizenship must be provided in the application. If you have dual citizenship, then you must indicate which citizenship will be printed on the certificate of registration.

<u>What is a specimen</u>?

A specimen is a sample of how you actually use the mark in commerce on your goods or with your services. A specimen shows the mark as your purchasers encounter it in the marketplace (e.g., on your labels or on your website).

<u>What is a drawing</u>?

The "drawing" is a clear image of the mark applicant seeks to register. The USPTO uses the drawing to upload the mark into the USPTO search database and to print the mark in the Official Gazette and on the registration certificate. There are two types of drawings: "standard character" and "special form."

<u>Can you register the name of a musical group or band</u>?

A band name may function as a service mark for "entertainment services in the nature of performances by a musical group" if it is used to identify live performances.

<u>What can I do to help the application proceed as smoothly as possible</u>?

1. File the application and all other documents electronically through theTEAS.

2. Carefully review all documents before filing to make sure all issues have been addressed and all the necessary elements are included.

3. Authorize email correspondence and promptly inform the USPTO of any change in correspondence address, including your email address. This can be done through TEAS.

4. Check the status of your application every 3-4 months using the Trademark Status and Document Retrieval (TSDR) system. If the USPTO has taken any action, you may need to respond promptly. All USPTO actions are available for viewing using the TSDR system.

How long does a trademark registration last?

The registration is valid as long as you timely file all post registration maintenance documents. You must file a "Declaration of Use under Section 8" between the fifth- and sixth year following registration. In addition, you must file a combined "Declaration of Use and Application for Renewal under Sections 8 and 9" between the ninth and tenth year after registration, and every 10 years thereafter. If these documents are not timely filed, your registration will be cancelled and cannot be revived or reinstated.

Where should I place the ® symbol?

There are no specific requirements on where the "®" symbol should be placed relative to the mark, but most businesses use the symbol in the upper right corner of the mark. The "®" symbol indicates that you have federally registered your trademark with the United States Patent and Trademark Office. It puts the public on notice that your mark is registered and that you have nationwide rights to it. You may only use the registration symbol with the mark on or in connection with the goods/services listed in the federal trademark registration and while the registration is still alive, (you may not continue to use it if you do not maintain the registration, or it expires). Note: Because several foreign countries use "®" to indicate that a mark is registered in that country, use of the symbol by the holder of a foreign registration may be proper.

Are there any restrictions on use of the "®" symbol?

There are three important restrictions on use of the "®" symbol: (1) it may only be used after the mark is registered (you may not use it during the application process); (2) it may only be used on or in connection with the goods and services listed in the federal registration; and (3) it may only be used while the registration is still alive (you may not continue to use it if you don't maintain the registration or it expires). Note: Because several foreign countries use "®" to indicate that a mark is registered in that country, use of the symbol by the holder of a foreign registration may be proper.

Is a federal registration valid outside of the United States?

No. However, certain countries recognize a United States registration as a basis for filing an application to register a mark in those countries under international treaties.

What if someone else is using my registered mark on related goods and services?

You may challenge the use of your trademark by someone else in several ways, depending on the factual situation. You should consider contacting an attorney specializing in trademark law. Local bar associations and phone directories usually have attorney listings broken down by specialties. Time can be of the essence.

My spouse owned a trademark registration and had since died. Do I own it now?

Perhaps. Because this depends on state law, the USPTO cannot provide a definite answer for all factual situations. You should consider contacting an attorney. Local bar associations and phone directories usually have attorney listings.

What is copyright?

Copyright is a form of protection grounded in the U.S. Constitution and granted by law for original works of authorship fixed in a tangible medium of expression. It covers both published and unpublished works.

How do I get copyright protection? Register on www.copyright.gov.

What does copyright protect?

Copyright protects original works of authorship including literary, dramatic, musical, and artistic works, such as poetry, novels, movies, songs, computer software, and architecture. Copyright does not protect facts, ideas, systems, or methods of operation, although it may protect the way these things are expressed.

How is a copyright different from a patent or a trademark?

Copyright protects original works of authorship, while a patent protects inventions or discoveries. Ideas and discoveries are not protected by copyright law, although the way in which they are expressed may be. A trademark protects words, phrases, symbols, or designs identifying the source of the goods or services of one party and distinguishing their work from those of others.

When is my work protected?

Your work is under copyright protection the moment it is created and fixed in a tangible form that is perceptible directly or with the aid of a machine or device.

Do I have to register with your office to be protected?

No. In general, registration is voluntary. Copyright exists from the moment the work is created. You will have to register, however, if you wish to bring a lawsuit for infringement of a U.S. work.

Why should I register my work if copyright protection is automatic?

Registration is recommended for a number of reasons. Many choose to register their works because they wish to have the facts of their copyright on the public record and have a certificate of registration. Registered works may be eligible for statutory damages and attorney's fees in successful litigation. Finally, if registration occurs within 5 years of publication, it is considered *prima facie* evidence in a court of law.

I have heard about a "poor man's copyright." What is it?

The practice of sending a copy of your own work to yourself is sometimes called a "poor man's copyright." There is no provision in the copyright law for this protection.

Is my copyright good in other countries?

The United States has copyright relations with most countries throughout the world, and as a result of these agreements, we honor each other citizens' copyrights. However, the U.S. does not have such copyright relationships with every country.

What does copyright protect?

Copyright protects original works of authorship including literary, dramatic, musical, and artistic works, such as poetry, novels, movies, songs, computer software, and architecture. Copyright does not protect facts, ideas, systems, or methods of operation, although it may protect these things in tangible form."

Can I copyright my website?

The original authorship appearing on a website may be protected by copyright. This includes writings, artwork, photographs, and other forms of authorship protected by copyright.

Can I copyright my domain name?

Copyright law does not protect domain names.

The Internet Corporation for Assigned Names and Numbers (ICANN), a nonprofit organization has assumed the responsibility for domain name system management, administers the assignation of domain names through accredited registers.

Can I copyright my recipe?

A mere listing of ingredients is not protected under copyright law. However, where a recipe or formula is accompanied by substantial literary expression in the form of an explanation or directions, or when there is a collection of recipes as in a cookbook, there may be a basis for copyright protection. Note that if you have secret ingredients to a recipe that you do not wish to be revealed, you should not submit your recipe for registration - applications and deposit copies are public records.

Can I copyright the name of my band?

Copyright law does not protect names. Sometimes under trademark law.

Can I copyright a name, title, slogan, or logo?

Copyright does not protect names, titles, slogans, or short phrases. In some cases, these things may be protected as trademarks. Contact the USPTO, 800-786-9199, for further information.

Copyright protection may be available for logo artwork that contains sufficient authorship. An artistic logo may also be protected as a trademark.

Can I copyright my idea?

Copyright does not protect ideas, concepts, systems, or methods of doing something. You may express your ideas in writing or drawings and claim copyright in your description but be aware that copyright will not protect the idea itself.

Does my work have to be published to be protected?

Publication is not necessary for copyright protection.

Can I register a diary I found in my grandmother's attic?

You can register copyright in the diary only if you own the rights to the work, for example, by will or by inheritance. Copyright is the right of the author of the work or the author's heirs or assignees, not of the one who only owns or possesses the physical work itself.

How do I protect my sighting of Elvis?

Copyright law does not protect sightings. However, copyright law will protect your photo (or other depiction) of your sighting of Elvis. File your claim to copyright online by means of the electronic Copyright Office (eCO). Pay the fee online and attach a copy of your photo. Alternatively, go to the Copyright Office website, fill in Form CO, print it, and mail it together with your photo and fee. No one can lawfully use your photo of your sighting, although someone else may file his own photo of his sighting. Copyright law protects the original photograph.

Can I get a star named after me and claim copyright to it?

No. There is a lot of misunderstanding about this. Names are not protected by copyright. Publishers of publications such as a star registry may register a claim to copyright in the text of the volume [or book] containing the names the registry has assigned to stars, and perhaps the compilation of data; but such a registration would not extend protection to any of the individual star names appearing therein. Copyright registration of such a volume of star names does not confer any official or governmental status on any of the star names included in the volume.

How do I register my copyright?

To register a work, submit a completed application form, a nonrefundable filing fee, which is $35 if you register online or $50 if you register using Form CO; and a nonreturnable copy or copies of the work to be registered.

What is the registration fee?

If you file online using eCO eService, the fee is $35 per application. If you file using Form CO, the fee is $50 per application. Each work requires a separate application.

Do you take credit cards?

If you file your application online using eCO eService, you may pay by credit card. Credit cards are not accepted for registration through the mail but may be used for registrations that are filed in person in the Copyright Office.

Do I have to send in my work? Do I get it back?

Yes, you must send the required copy or copies of the work to be registered. Your copies will not be returned. If you register online using eCO eService, you may attach an electronic copy of your deposit. However, even if you register online, if the Library of Congress requires a hard-copy deposit of your work, you must send what the Library defines as the "best edition" of your work.

May I register more than one work on one application? Where do I list the titles?

You may register unpublished works as a collection on one application with one title for the complete collection if certain conditions are met. It is not necessary to list the individual titles in your collection. Published works may only be registered as a collection if they were actually first published as a collection and if other requirements have been met.

Do I have to use my real name on the form? Can I use a stage or a pen name?

There is no legal requirement that the author be identified by his or her real name on the application form. If filing under a fictitious name, check the "Pseudonymous" box when giving information about the authors.

Will my personal information be available to the public?

Please be aware that when you register your claim to a copyright in a work with the U.S. Copyright Office, it is a public record. All the information you provide on your copyright registration is available to the public and will be available on the Internet.

How long does the registration process take, and when will I receive my certificate?

The time the Copyright Office requires to process an application varies, depending on the number of applications the Office is receiving and clearing at the time of submission and the extent of questions associated with the application.

Can I submit my manuscript on a computer disk?

No. Floppy disks and other removal media such as Zip disks, except for CD-ROMs, are not acceptable. Therefore, the Copyright Office still generally requires a printed copy or audio recording of the work for deposit. However, if you register online using eCO eService, you may attach an electronic copy of your deposit. However, even if you register online, if the Library of Congress requires a hard-copy deposit of your work, you must send what the Library defines as the "best edition" of your work.

Can I submit a CD-ROM of my work?

Yes. The deposit requirement consists of the best edition of the CD-ROM package for any work, including the accompanying operating software, instruction manual, and a printed version, when/if you are including it with the package.

Does my work have to be published to be protected?

Publication is not necessary for copyright protection.

How much do I have to change in my own work to make a new claim of copyright?

You may make a new claim in your work if the changes are substantial and creative, something more than just editorial changes or minor changes. This would qualify as a new derivative work. For instance, simply making spelling corrections throughout a work does not warrant a new registration but adding an additional chapter would.

Do you have special mailing requirements?

If you register online, you may attach an electronic copy of your deposit unless a hard-copy deposit is required under the "Best Edition" requirements of the Library of Congress. If you file using a paper application, our only requirement is that all three elements—the application, the copy, or copies of the work together with the shipping slip printed when you fill out Form CO online, and the filing fee—be sent in the same package. Please limit any individual box to twenty pounds. Many people send their material to us by certified mail, with a return receipt request.

What Form Do I Fill Out to Register My Copyright?

Online registration through the eCO is the preferred way to register basic claims. The next best option for registering basic claims is the new fill-in Form CO. Using 2-D barcode scanning technology, the Office can process these forms much faster and more efficiently than paper forms completed manually. Complete Form CO, print it out, and mail it along with a check or money order and your deposit. Do not save your filled-out Form CO and reuse it for another registration. The 2-D barcode it contains is unique for each work that you register for.

Paper versions of Form TX (literary works); Form VA (visual arts works); Form PA; (perform arts); Form SR (sound recordings) are available on the Copyright Office website. However, staff will send them to you by postal mail upon request. Remember that online registration through eCO and fill-in Form CO can also be used.

Can I obtain a copyright of my business name?

Names, titles, short phrases, and slogans are not eligible for copyright protection. However, you may have protection under the federal trademark protection laws.

How long does a copyright last?

The term of copyright for a particular work depends on several factors, including whether it has been published, and, if so, the date of first publication. As a general rule, for works created after January 1, 1978, copyright protection lasts for the life of the author plus an additional 70 years. For an anonymous work, a pseudonymous work, or a work made for hire, the copyright endures for a term of 95 years from the year of its first publication or a term of 120 years from the year of its creation, whichever expires first.

Do I have to renew my copyright?

No. Works created on or after January 1, 1978, are not subject to renewal registration. As to works published or registered prior to January 1, 1978, renewal registration is optional after 28 years but does provide certain legal advantages. For works first published prior to 1978, the term will vary depending on several factors.

Can I get permission to use the work of another?

You can ask for it. If you know who the copyright owner is, you may contact the owner directly. If you are not certain about the ownership or have other related questions, you may wish to request that the Copyright Office conduct a search of its records, or you may search yourself. See the next question for more details.

How can I find out who owns a copyright?

We can provide you with the information available in our records. A search of registrations, renewals, and recorded transfers of ownership made before 1978 requires a manual search of our files. Upon request, our staff will search our records at the statutory rate of $165 for each hour (2 hours minimum). There is no fee if you conduct a search in person at the Copyright Office. Copyright registrations and documents recorded from 1978 to date are available for searching online.

How much of someone else's work can I use without getting permission?

Under the *fair use* doctrine of the U.S. copyright statute, it is permissible to use limited portions of a work including quotes, for purposes such as commentary, criticism, news reporting, and scholarly reports. There are no legal rules permitting the use of a specific number of words, a certain number of musical notes, or percentage of a work. Whether a particular use qualifies as fair use depends on all the circumstances.

How much do I have to change to claim copyright in someone else's work?

Only the owner of copyright in a work has the right to prepare, or to authorize someone else to create, a recent version of that work. Accordingly, you cannot claim copyright to another's work, no matter how much you change it, unless you have the owner's consent.

Somebody infringed my copyright. What can I do?

A party may seek to protect his or her copyrights against unauthorized use by filing a civil lawsuit in federal district court. If you believe that your copyright has been infringed, consult an attorney. In cases of willful infringement for profit, the U.S. Attorney may initiate a criminal investigation.

Could I be sued for using somebody else's work, quotes, or samples?

If you use a copyrighted work without authorization, the owner may be entitled to bring an infringement action against you. There are circumstances under the fair use doctrine where a quote or a sample may be used without permission. However, in case of doubt, the Copyright Office recommends that permission be obtained.

Do you have a list of songs or movies in the public domain?

No, we neither compile nor maintain such a list. A search of our records, however, may reveal whether a particular work has fallen into the public domain. We will conduct a search of our records by the title of a work, an author's name, or a claimant's name. Upon request, our staff will search for our records at the statutory rate of $165 for each hour (2 hours minimum). You may also search the records in person without paying a fee.

Can a school show a movie without permission from the copyright owner?

If the movie is for entertainment purposes, you need to get a clearance or license for its performance.

It is not necessary to obtain permission if you show the movie in the course of "face-to-face teaching activities" in a nonprofit educational institution, in a classroom or similar place devoted to instruction if the copy of the movie being performed is a lawful copy. This exemption encompasses instructional activities relating to a wide variety of subjects, but it does not include performances for recreation or entertainment purposes, even if there is cultural value or intellectual appeal.

My local copying store will not make reproductions of old family photographs. What can I do?

Photocopying shops, photography stores and other photo developing stores are often reluctant to make reproductions of old photographs for fear of violating the copyright law and being sued. These fears are reasonable, because copy shops have been sued for reproducing copyrighted works and have been required to pay substantial damages for infringing copyrighted works. The policy established by a shop is a business decision and risk assessment that the business is entitled to make, because the business may face liability if they reproduce a work even if they did not know the work was copyrighted.

Trade Secrets

Any valuable commercial information that provides a business with an advantage over competitors who do not have that information. In most states, a trade secret may consist of any formula, pattern, physical device, idea, process, or compilation of information that both:

- Provides the owner of the information with a competitive advantage in the marketplace and is treated in a way that can be expected to prevent the public or competitors from learning about it, absent improper acquisition, or theft.

Some examples of potential trade secrets are:

- a formula for a sports drink; survey methods used by professional pollsters; recipes; an invention for which a patent application has not yet been filed; marketing strategies; manufacturing techniques, and computer algorithms.

Unlike other forms of intellectual property such as patents, copyrights and trademarks, trade secrecy is a do-it-yourself form of protection. You do not register with the government to secure your trade secret; you simply keep the information confidential. Trade secret protection lasts for as long as the secret is kept confidential. Once a trade secret is made available to the public, trade secret protection ends.

What types of information can trade secrets protect?

Trade secrets often protect valuable technical information that cannot be sheltered under other forms of intellectual property law, such as the formula for Coca-Cola. Trade secrets may also:

- protect ideas that offer a business a competitive advantage, thereby enabling a company or individual to get a head start on the competition -- for example, an idea for a new type of product or a new website; keep competitors from learning that a product or service is under development and from discovering its functional or technical attributes -- for example, how a new software program works; protect valuable business information such as marketing plans, cost and price information and customer lists -- for example, a company's plans to launch a new product line; protect "negative know-how" -- that is, information you've learned during the course of research and development on what not to do or what does not work optimally -- for example, research revealing that a new type of drug is ineffective, or protect any other information that has some value and is not generally known by your competitors -- for example, a list of customers ranked by how profitable their business is.

What rights does the owner of a trade secret have?

A trade secret owner can prevent the following groups of people from copying, using, or benefiting from its trade secrets or disclosing them to others without permission:

- people who are automatically bound by a duty of confidentiality not to disclose or use trade secret information, including any employee who routinely comes into contact with the employer's trade secrets as part of the employee's job; people who acquire a trade secret through improper means such as theft, industrial espionage or bribery; people who knowingly obtain trade secrets from people who have no right to disclose them; people who learn about a trade secret by accident or mistake, but had reason to know that the information was a protected trade secret, and people who sign nondisclosure agreements (also known as "confidentiality agreements") promising not to disclose trade secrets without authorization from the owner. This may be the best way for a trade secret owner to establish a duty of confidentiality, such as Nondisclosure Agreements. How can a business protect its trade secrets?

How can a business protect its trade secrets?

Simply calling information a trade secret will not make it so and the business must affirmatively behave in a way that proves its desire to keep the information secret, and some companies will go to extreme lengths to do so.

Ex. The formula for Coca-Cola, perhaps the world's most famous trade secret, is kept locked in a bank vault that can be opened only by a resolution of the Coca-Cola Company's board of directors. Only two Coca-Cola employees ever know the formula at the same time; their identities are never disclosed to the public and they are not allowed to fly on the same airplane.

What is a patent?

A patent for an invention is the grant of a property right to the inventor, issued by the United States Patent and Trademark Office. The term of a new patent is 20 years from the date on which the application for the patent was filed in the United States or, in special cases, from the date an earlier related application was filed, subject to the payment of maintenance fees. U.S. patent grants are effective only within the United States, U.S. territories, and U.S. possessions. Under certain circumstances, patent term extensions or adjustments may be available.

The right conferred by the patent grant is, in the language of the statute and of the grant itself, "the right to exclude others from making, using, offering for sale, or selling" the invention in the United States or "importing" the invention into the United States. What is granted is not the right to make, use, offer for sale, sell, or import, but the right to exclude others from making, using, offering for sale, selling, or importing the invention. Once a patent is issued, the patentee must enforce the patent without aid of the USPTO.

There are three types of patents:

Utility patents may be granted to anyone who invents or discovers any new and useful process, machine, article of manufacture, or composition of matter, or any new and useful improvement thereof;

Design patents may be granted to anyone who invents a new, original, and ornamental design for an article of manufacture; and

Plant patents may be granted to anyone who invents or discovers and asexually reproduces any distinct and new variety of plant.

What types of things can be patented?

The patent law specifies the general field of subject matter that can be patented and the conditions under which a patent may be obtained.

In the language of the statute, any person who "invents or discovers any new and useful process, machine, manufacture, or composition of matter, or any new and useful improvement thereof, may obtain a patent," subject to the conditions and requirements of the law. The word "process" is defined by law as a process, act, or method, and primarily includes industrial or technical processes. The term "machine" used in the statute needs no explanation. The term "manufacture" refers to articles that are made and includes all manufactured articles. The term "composition of matter" relates to chemical compositions and may include mixtures of ingredients as well as new chemical compounds. These classes of subject matter taken together include everything that is made by man and the processes for making the products.

The patent law specifies that the subject matter must be "useful." The term "useful" in this connection refers to the condition that the subject matter has a useful purpose and includes how it operates, that is, a machine, which will not operate to perform the intended purpose, would not be called useful, and therefore would not be granted a patent.

<u>Can an idea obtain a patent</u>?

A patent cannot be obtained upon a mere idea or suggestion. The patent is granted upon the new machine, manufacture, etc., as has been said, and not upon the idea or suggestion of the new machine. A complete description of the actual machine or other subject matter for which a patent is sought is required.

What are the conditions for obtaining a patent?

In order for an invention to be patentable it must be new as defined in the patent law, which provides that an invention cannot be patented if: "(a) the invention was known or used by others in this country, or patented or described in a printed publication in this or a foreign country, before the invention thereof by the applicant for patent," or "(b) the invention was patented or described in a printed publication in this or a foreign country or in public use or on sale in this country more than one year prior to the application for patent in the United States."

Do I need an attorney?

The preparation of an application for patent and the conducting of the proceedings in the United States Patent and Trademark Office (USPTO or Office) to obtain the patent is an undertaking requiring the knowledge of patent law and rules and Office practice and procedures, as well as knowledge of the scientific or technical matters involved in the invention. Inventors may prepare their own applications and file them in the USPTO and conduct the proceedings themselves, but unless they are familiar with these matters or study them in detail, they may get into considerable difficulty. While a patent may be obtained in many cases by persons not skilled in this work, there would be no assurance that the patent obtained would protect the particular invention.

The USPTO has the power to disbar, or suspend from practicing before it, persons guilty of gross misconduct, etc., but this can only be done after a full hearing with the presentation of clear and convincing evidence concerning the misconduct. The USPTO will receive and, in appropriate cases, act upon complaints against attorneys and agents. The fees charged to inventors by patent attorneys and agents for their professional services are not subject to regulation by the USPTO. Definite evidence of overcharging may provide a basis for USPTO action, but the Office rarely intervenes in disputes concerning fees.

How do I protect my patent internationally?

Since the rights granted by a U.S. patent extend only throughout the territory of the United States and have no effect in a foreign country, an inventor who wishes patent protection in other countries must apply for a patent in each of the other countries or in regional patent offices. Every country has its own patent law, and a person desiring a patent in a particular country must make an application for patent in that country, in accordance with the requirements of that country. There is a treaty relating to patents, which is adhered to by 168 countries, including the United States, and is known as the Paris Convention for the Protection of Industrial Property. It provides that each country guarantees the citizens of the other countries the same rights in patent and trademark matters that it gives to its own citizens.

What other treaties protect patents?

Another treaty, known as the Patent Cooperation Treaty, was negotiated at a diplomatic conference in Washington, D.C., in June of 1970. The treaty came into force on January 24, 1978. It is presently (as of December 14, 2004) adhered to by over 124 countries, including the United States. The treaty facilitates the filing of applications for patents on the same invention in member countries by providing, among other things, centralized filing procedures and a standardized application format.

Is stealing trade secrets a crime?

Every state has a law prohibiting theft or disclosure of trade secrets. Most of these laws are derived from the Uniform Trade Secrets Act (UTSA), drafted by legal scholars.

Intentional theft of trade secrets can constitute a crime under both federal and state laws. The most significant federal law dealing with trade secret theft is the Economic Espionage Act of 1996 (EEA) (18 U.S.C., Sections 1831 to 1839). The EEA gives the U.S. Attorney General sweeping powers to prosecute any person or company involved in trade secret misappropriation and punishes intentional stealing, copying, or receiving of trade secrets. Penalties for violations are severe: Individuals may be fined up to $500,000 and corporations up to $5 million. A violator may also be sent to prison for up to ten years. All property used and proceeds derived from the theft can be seized and sold by the government. The EEA applies not only to thefts that occur within the United States, but also to thefts outside the U.S. if the thief is a U.S. citizen or corporation, or if any act in furtherance of the offense occurred in the U.S. If the theft is performed on behalf of a foreign government or agent, the corporate fines can double, and jail time may increase to 15 years.

Several states have also enacted laws making trade secret infringement a crime. For example, in California it is a crime to acquire, disclose or use trade secrets without authorization. Violators may be fined up to $5,000, sentenced to one year in jail, or both.

What are the symbols used for IP?

Patent Pending:

- means a patent application has been filed.
- the application can be a regular, non-provisional application, or a provisional application.
- does not mean a patent is certain to be issued.
- is a warning that a patent might be issued?

The ™ sign:

- flags an unregistered trademark.
- usually superscripted or subscripted
- expresses the owner's belief and/or intention.
- (Trademarks are brand names for products)

The ^SM^ sign:

- flags an unregistered service mark.
- usually superscripted or subscripted
- expresses the owner's belief and/or intention.
- service marks are brand names for services.

The ® symbol:

- flags a federally registered trademark or service mark.
- cannot be used unless the mark is federally registered.
- indicates USPTO validation of mark.
- usually superscripted or subscripted
- replaces either the TM or SM sign when the mark is registered.

The © symbol:

- first element of copyright notice
- word "Copyright" can be used instead.
- followed by year date of publication and the owner's name.
- used whether or not work has a copyright registration.
- copyright notice not required, but highly recommended.

False Advertising

"Any advertising or promotion that misrepresents the nature, characteristics, qualities or geographic origin of goods, services or commercial activities. (Lanham Act)"

What is required to prove false advertising?

To establish that an advertisement is false, a plaintiff must prove five things: (1) a false statement of fact has been made about the advertiser's own or another person's goods, services, or commercial activity; (2) the statement either deceives or has the potential to deceive a substantial portion of its targeted audience; (3) the deception is also likely to affect the purchasing decisions of its audience; (4) the advertising involves goods or services in interstate commerce; and (5) the deception has either resulted in or is likely to result in injury to the plaintiff. The most heavily weighed factor is the advertisement's potential to injure a customer. The injury is usually attributed to money the consumer lost through a purchase that would not have been made had the advertisement not been misleading. False statements can be defined in two ways: those that are false on their face and those that are implicitly false.

What regulations exist against false advertising?

One early attempt to create advertising industry standards was made in 1911 when the trade journal *Printer's Ink* proposed that false advertising be classified as a crime. As a result, false advertising became a misdemeanor in forty-four states. Statutes were based on the model statute suggested by *Printer's Ink*. These statutes are still in effect; however, they are rarely used because it requires proving that the false advertising exists "beyond a reasonable doubt" a difficult standard to meet.

In place of the *Printer's Ink* statute, states adopted the Uniform Deceptive Trade Practices Act of 1964 (revised 1966), which lists a dozen different items that are prohibited in the advertising trade. The only remedy available under this act is injunctive relief—a court order that admonishes the guilty party for its actions—, which may explain the small number of states that have adopted it. (As of 2003, only twelve states have adopted the statute in some form.) Other states have different statutes regarding false advertising. Most of these statutes require the courts to interpret state laws using federal guidelines provided by the Federal Trade Commission (FTC). According to the FTC, which amended its standards to help regulate cigarette labeling, three elements are necessary to show that an advertisement is false or unfair. The ad has to offend public policy; be immoral, unethical, oppressive, or unscrupulous; and substantially injure consumers.

What are the types of false advertising?

Today's regulations define three main acts that constitute false advertising: failure to disclose, flawed and insignificant research, and product disparagement. The majority of these regulations are outlined in the Lanham Act, which contains the statutes that govern TRADEMARK law in the U.S.

Failure to Disclose It is considered false advertising under the Lanham Act if a representation is "untrue as a result of the failure to disclose a material fact." Therefore, false advertising can come from both misstatements and partially correct statements that are misleading because they do not disclose something the consumer should know. The Trademark Law Revision Act of 1988, which added several amendments to the Lanham Act, left creation of the line between sufficient and insufficient disclosure to the discretion of the courts.

American Home Products Corp. v. Johnson & Johnson, N.Y. 1987 is an example of how the courts use their discretion in determining when a disclosure is insufficient. In this case, Johnson and Johnson advertised a drug by comparing its side effects to those of a similar American Home Products drug, leaving out a few of its own side effects in the process. Although the Lanham Act does not require full disclosure, the court held the defendant to a higher standard and ruled the advertisement misleading because of the potential health risks it posed to consumers.

Flawed and Insignificant Research Advertisements based on flawed and insignificant research are defined under section 43(a) of the Lanham Act "as representations found to be unsupported by accepted authority or research or which are contradicted by prevailing authority or research." These advertisements are false on their face.

Product Disparagement Product disparagement involves discrediting a competitor's product. The 1988 amendment to the Lanham Act extends claims for false advertising to misrepresentations about another's products.

What are the remedies for false advertising?

Injunctive Relief Injunctive relief is granted by the courts upon the satisfaction of two requirements. First, a plaintiff must demonstrate a "likelihood of deception or confusion on the part of the buying public caused by a product's false or misleading description or advertising." Second, a plaintiff must demonstrate that "irreparable harm" has been inflicted, even if such harm is a decrease in sales that cannot be completely attributed to a defendant's false advertising. It is virtually impossible to prove that sales can or will be damaged; therefore, the plaintiff only has to establish that there exists a causal relationship between a decline in its sales and a competitor's false advertising. Furthermore, if a competitor specifically names the plaintiff's product in a false or misleading advertisement, the harm will be presumed. (McNeil, Inc. v. American Home Products Corp., 1988).

Corrective Advertising Corrective advertising can be ruled in two separate ways. First, and most commonly, the court can require a defendant to launch a corrective advertising campaign and to make an affirmative, correcting statement in that campaign. For example, in *Alpo*, the court required Purina to distribute a corrective release to all of those who had received the initial, false information.

Second, the courts can award a plaintiff monetary damage so that the plaintiff can conduct a corrective advertising campaign to counter the defendant's false advertisements. For example, in U-Haul International v. Jartran, Inc.,1986, the plaintiff, U-Haul International, was awarded $13.6 million— the cost of its corrective advertising campaign. To collect damages, the plaintiff has to show either that some consumers were actually deceived or that the defendant used false advertising in bad faith.

Four types of damages are awarded for false advertising: profits the plaintiff loses when sales are diverted to the false advertiser; profits lost by the plaintiff on sales made at prices reduced as a demonstrated result of the false advertising; the cost of any advertising that actually and reasonably responds to the defendant's offending advertisements; and quantifiable harm to the plaintiff's good will to the extent that complete and corrective advertising hasn't repaired that harm.

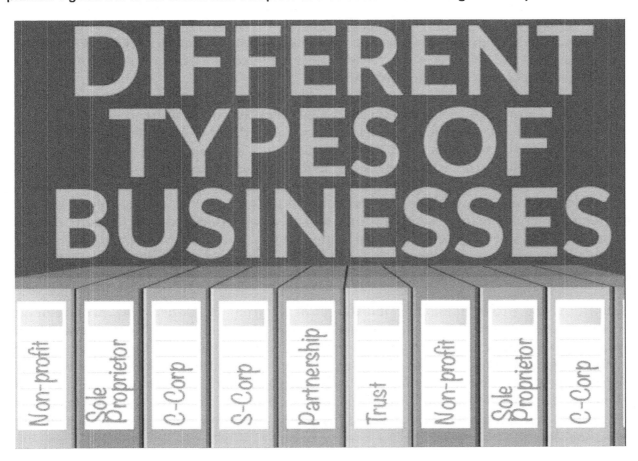

A business entity is an organization created by one or more natural persons to execute a trade or business. ... Types of business entities include corporations, partnerships, limited liability companies, limited liability partnerships.

Sole Proprietorship

A business that legally has no separate existence from its owner. Income and losses are taxed on the individual's personal income tax return.

The sole proprietorship is the simplest business form under which one can operate a business. The sole proprietorship is not a legal entity. It simply refers to a person who owns the business and is personally responsible for its debts. A sole proprietorship can operate under the name of its owner, or it can do business under a fictitious name, such as d.b.a (doing business as) Cardi O's Nail Salon. The fictitious name is simply a trade name--it does not create a legal entity separate from the sole proprietor owner.

The sole proprietorship is a popular business form due to its simplicity, ease of setup, and nominal cost. A sole proprietor need only register his or her name and secure local licenses, and the sole proprietor is ready for business. A distinct disadvantage, however, is that the owner of the sole proprietorship remains personally liable for all the business's debts. Therefore, if a sole proprietor business runs into financial trouble, creditors can bring lawsuits against the business owner. If such suits are successful, the owner will have to pay the business debts with his or her own money.

The owner of a sole proprietorship typically signs contracts in his or her own name because the sole proprietorship has no separate identity under the law. The sole proprietor owner will typically have customers write checks in the owner's name, even if the business uses a fictitious name. Sole proprietor owners can, and often do, commingle personal and business property and funds, something that partnerships, LLCs and corporations cannot do. Sole proprietorships often have their bank accounts in the name of the owner. Sole proprietors need not observe formalities such as voting, and meetings associated with the more complex business forms. Sole proprietorships can bring lawsuits (and can be sued) using the name of the sole proprietor owner. Many businesses begin as sole proprietorships and graduate to more complex business forms as the business develops.

Because a sole proprietorship is indistinguishable from its owner, sole proprietorship taxation is quite simple. The income earned by a sole proprietorship is income earned by its owner. A sole proprietor reports the sole proprietorship income and/or losses and expenses by filling out and filing a Schedule C, along with the standard Form 1040. Your profits and losses are first recorded on a tax form called Schedule C, which is filed along with your 1040. Then the "bottom-line amount" from Schedule C is transferred to your personal tax return. This aspect is attractive because business losses you suffer may offset income earned from other sources.

As the sole proprietor, you must also file a Schedule SE with Form 1040. You use Schedule SE to calculate how much self-employment tax you owe. You need not pay unemployment tax on yourself, although you must pay unemployment tax on any employees of the business. Of course, you will not enjoy unemployment benefits should the business suffer.

Sole proprietors are personally liable for all debts of a sole proprietorship business. Let us examine this more closely because the potential liability can be alarming. Assume that the sole proprietor borrows money to operate but the business loses its major customer, goes out of business, and is unable to repay the loan. The sole proprietor is liable for the amount of the loan, which can potentially consume all her personal assets.

Imagine an even worse scenario: The sole proprietor (or even one her employees) participates in a business-related accident in which someone is injured or killed. The resulting negligence case can be brought against the sole proprietor owner and against her personal assets, such as her bank account, her retirement accounts, and even her home.

If another party wrongs the sole proprietor, he can bring a lawsuit in his own name. Conversely, if another party wrongs a corporation or LLC, the entity must bring its claim under the name of the company.

The advantages of a sole proprietorship include:

- Owners can establish a sole proprietorship instantly, easily, and inexpensively.
- Sole proprietorships carry little, if any, ongoing formalities.
- A sole proprietor need not pay unemployment tax on himself or herself (although he or she must pay unemployment tax on employees).
- Owners may freely mix business or personal assets.

The disadvantages of a sole proprietorship include:

- Owners are subject to unlimited personal liability for the debts, losses, and liabilities of the business.
- Owners cannot raise capital by selling an interest in the business.
- Sole proprietorships rarely survive the death or incapacity of their owners and so do not retain value.

Partnership

Definition: *A legal form of business operation between two or more individuals who share management and profits. The federal government recognizes several types of partnerships. The two most common are general and limited partnerships.*

If your business is owned and operated by several individuals, you will want to look at structuring your business as a partnership. Partnerships come in two varieties: general partnerships and limited partnerships. In a general partnership, the partners manage the company and assume responsibility for the partnership's debts and other obligations. A limited partnership has both general and limited partners. The general partners own and operate the business and assume liability for the partnership, while the limited partners serve as investors only; they have no control over the company and are not subject to the same liabilities as the general partners.

Unless you expect to have many passive investors, limited partnerships are not the best choice for a new business because of all the required filings and administrative complexities. If you have two or more partners who want to be actively involved, a general partnership would be much easier to form.

One of the major advantages of a partnership is the tax treatment it enjoys. A partnership does not pay tax on its income but "passes through" any profits or losses to the individual partners. At tax time, the partnership must file a tax return (Form 1065) that reports its income and loss to the IRS. In addition, each partner reports his or her share of income and loss on Schedule K-1 of Form 1065.

Personal liability is a major concern if you use a general partnership to structure your business. Like sole proprietors, general partners are personally liable for the partnership's obligations and debts. Each general partner can act on behalf of the partnership, take out loans and make decisions that will affect and be binding on all the partners (if the partnership agreement permits). Keep in mind that partnerships are also more expensive to establish than sole proprietorships because they require more legal and accounting services.

If you decide to organize your business as a partnership, be sure you draft a partnership agreement (a CONTRACT!) that details how business decisions are made, how disputes are resolved and how to oversee a buyout. The contract should address the purpose of the business and the authority and responsibility of each partner. It is a good idea to consult an attorney experienced with small businesses for help in drafting the agreement. Here are some other issues you will want the contract to address:

- How will the ownership interest be shared? It is not necessary, for example, for two owners to equally share ownership and authority. However, if you decide to do it, make sure the proportion is stated clearly in the agreement.
- How will decisions be made? It is a clever idea to establish voting rights in case a major disagreement arises. When just two partners own the business 50-50, there is the possibility of a deadlock. To avoid this, some businesses provide in advance for a third partner, a trusted associate who may own only 1 percent of the business but whose vote can break a tie.
- When one partner withdraws, how will the purchase price be determined? One possibility is to agree on a neutral third party, such as your banker or accountant, to find an appraiser to determine the price of the partnership interest.
- If a partner withdraws from the partnership, when will the money be paid? Depending on the partnership agreement, you can agree that the money be paid over three, five or ten years, with interest. You do not want to be hit with a cash-flow crisis if the entire price has to be paid on the spot in one lump sum.

Sub-chapter S Corp.

Definition: A special form of corporation that allows the protection of limited liability but direct flow-through of profits and losses.

The S corporation is often more attractive to small-business owners than a standard (or C) corporation. That is because an S corporation has some appealing tax benefits and still provides business owners with the liability protection of a corporation. With an S corporation, income and losses are passed through to shareholders and included in their individual tax returns. As a result, there is just one level of federal tax to pay.

A corporation must meet certain conditions to be eligible for a subchapter S election. First, the corporation must have no more than seventy-five shareholders. In calculating the 75-shareholder limit, spouses count as one shareholder. Also, only the following entities may be shareholders: individuals, estates, certain trusts, certain partnerships, tax-exempt charitable organizations, and other S corporations (but only if the other S corporation is the sole shareholder).

In addition, owners of S corporations who do not have inventory can use the cash method of accounting, which is simpler than the accrual method. Under this method, income is taxable when received and expenses are deductible when paid.

S corporations do come with some downsides. For example, S corporations are subject to make of the same requirements corporations must follow, and that means higher legal and tax service costs. They also must file articles of incorporation, hold directors and shareholders' meetings, keep corporate minutes, and allow shareholders to vote on major corporate decisions. The legal and accounting costs of setting up an S corporation are also similar to those for a standard corporation. Moreover, S corporations can only issue common stock, which can hamper capital-raising efforts.

An S corporation may revoke its subchapter S status by either failing to meet the conditions of eligibility for S corporations, or by filing with the IRS no later than two months and 15 days after the first day of the taxable year.

When it comes to choosing the best structure for a business, many entrepreneurs have trouble making a choice between S corporations and LLCs--that is most likely because they possess similarities: They offer their owners limited liability protection and are both pass-through tax entities. Pass-through taxation allows the income or loss generated by the business to be reflected on the personal income tax return of the owners. This special tax status eliminates any possibility of double taxation for S corporations and LLCs.

That is where the similarities end. The ownership of an S corporation is restricted to no more than seventy-five shareholders, whereas an LLC can have an unlimited number of members (owners). In addition, while an S corporation cannot have non-U.S. citizens as shareholders, an LLC can. In addition, S corporations cannot be owned by C corporations, other S corporations, many trusts, LLCs, or partnerships. LLCs are not subject to these restrictions.

LLCs are also more flexible in distributing profits than S corporations, wherein the corporation can only have one class of stock and your percentage of ownership determines the percentage of pass-through income. On the other hand, an LLC can have many different classes of interest, and the percentage of pass-through income is not tied to ownership percentage.

S corporations are not without their advantages, however. One person can form an S corporation, while in a few states at least two people are required to form an LLC. Existence is perpetual for S corporations. Conversely, LLCs typically have limited life spans.

The stock of S corporations is freely transferable, while the interest (ownership) of LLCs is not. This free transferability of interest means the shareholders of S corporations are able to sell their interest without obtaining the approval of the other shareholders. In contrast, members of LLCs would need the approval of the other members in order to sell their interest. Lastly, S corporations may be advantageous in terms of self-employment taxes in comparison to LLCs.

Limited Liability Company

Definition: *A form of business organization with the liability-shield advantages of a corporation and the flexibility and tax pass-through advantages of a partnership*

Many states allow a business form called the limited liability company (LLC). The LLC arose from business owners' desire to adopt a business structure permitting them to operate like a traditional partnership. Their goal was to distribute income to the partners (who reported it on their individual income tax returns) but also to protect themselves from personal liability for the business's debts, as with the corporate business form. In general, unless the business owner establishes a separate corporation, the owner, and partners (if any) assume complete liability for all debts of the business. Under the LLC rules, however, an individual is not responsible for the firm's debt, provided he or she did not secure them personally, as with a second mortgage, a personal credit card or by putting personal assets on the line.

The LLC offers a number of advantages over subchapter S corporations. For example, while S corporations can issue only one class of the company stock, LLCs can offer several different classes with different rights. In addition, S corporations are limited to a maximum of seventy-five individual shareholders (who must be U.S. residents), whereas an unlimited number of individuals, corporations, and partnerships may participate in an LLC.

The LLC also carries significant tax advantages over the limited partnership. For instance, unless the partner in a limited partnership assumes an active role, his or her losses are considered passive losses and cannot be used as tax deductions to offset active income. However, if the partner takes an active role in the firm's management, he or she becomes liable for the firm's debt. It is a catch-22 situation. The owners of an LLC, on the other hand, do not assume liability for the business' debt, and any losses the LLC incurs can be used as tax deductions against active income.

However, in exchange for these two considerable benefits, the owners of LLCs must meet the "transferability restriction test," which means the ownership interests in the LLC are not transferable without restriction. This restriction makes the LLC structure unworkable for major corporations. For corporations to attract large sums of capital, their corporate stock must be easily transferable to the stock exchanges. However, this restriction is not as problematic for smaller companies, where stock ownership transfers take place infrequently.

Since the LLC is a new legal form for businesses, federal and state governments are still looking at ways to tighten regulations concerning them. Unfortunately, some investment promoters use LLCs to evade securities laws. That is why it is imperative to consult with your attorney and CPA before deciding which corporate structure makes sense for your business.

Corporation

Definition: *A form of business operation that declares the business as a separate, legal entity guided by a group of officers known as the board of directors.*

A corporate structure is the most advantageous way to start a business because the corporation exists as a separate entity. In general, a corporation has all the legal rights of an individual, except for the right to vote and certain other limitations. Corporations are given the right to exist by the state that issues their charter. If you incorporate in one state to take advantage of liberal corporate laws but do business in another state, you will have to file for "qualification" in the state in which you wish to operate the business. There is usually a fee that must be paid to qualify to do business in a state.

You can incorporate your business by filing articles of incorporation with the appropriate agency in your state. Usually, only one corporation can have any given name in each state. After incorporation, stock is issued to the company's shareholders in exchange for the cash or other assets they transfer to it in return for that stock. Once a year, the shareholders elect the board of directors, who meet to discuss and guide corporate affairs anywhere from once a month to once a year.

Each year, the directors elect officers such as a president, secretary, and treasurer to conduct the day-to-day affairs of the corporate business. There also may be additional officers such as vice presidents if the directors so decide. Along with the articles of incorporation, the directors and shareholders usually adopt corporate bylaws that govern the powers and authority of the directors, officers, and shareholders.

Even small, private, professional corporations, such as a legal or dental practice, need to adhere to the principles that govern a corporation. For instance, upon incorporation, common stock needs to be distributed to the shareholders and a board of directors elected. If there is only one person forming the corporation, that person is the sole shareholder of stock in the corporation and can elect himself or herself to the board of directors as well as any other individuals that person deems appropriate.

Corporations, if properly formed, capitalized, and operated (including appropriate annual meetings of shareholders and directors) limit the liability of their shareholders. Even if the corporation is not successful or is held liable for damages in a lawsuit, the most a shareholder can lose is his or her investment in the stock. The shareholder's personal assets are not on the line for corporate liabilities.

Corporations file Form 1120 with the IRS and pay their own taxes. Salaries paid to shareholders who are employees of the corporation are deductible. Nevertheless, dividends paid to shareholders are not deductible and therefore do not reduce the corporation's tax liability. A corporation must end its tax year on December 31 if it derives its income primarily from personal services (such as dental care, legal counseling, business consulting and so on) provided by its shareholders.

If the corporation is small, the shareholders should prepare and sign a shareholders buy-sell agreement. This contract provides that if a shareholder dies or wants to sell his or her stock, it must first be offered to the surviving shareholders. It also may provide a method to determine the fair price that should be paid for those shares. Such agreements are usually funded with life insurance to purchase the stock of deceased shareholders.

If a corporation is large and sells its shares to many individuals, it may have to register with the Securities and Exchange Commission (SEC) or state regulatory bodies. More common is the corporation with only a few shareholders, which can issue its shares without any such registration under private offering exemptions. For a small corporation, responsibilities of the shareholders can be defined in the corporate minutes, and a shareholder who wants to leave can be accommodated without many legal hassles. In addition, until your small corporation has operated successfully for many years, you will still have to accept personal liability for any loans made by banks or other lenders to your corporation.

While some people feel that a corporation enhances the image of a small business, one disadvantage is the potential double taxation: The Corporation must pay taxes on its net income, and shareholders must pay taxes on any dividends received from the corporation. Business owners often increase their own salaries to reduce or wipe out corporate profits and thereby lower the possibility of having those profits taxed twice-once to the corporation and again to the shareholders upon receipt of dividends from the corporation.

Nonprofit Corporation

Definition: *A business organization that serves some public purpose and therefore enjoys special treatment under the law. Nonprofit corporations, contrary to their name, can make a profit but cannot be designed primarily for profit making.*

When it comes to your business structure, have you thought about organizing your venture as a nonprofit corporation? Unlike a for-profit business, a nonprofit may be eligible for certain benefits, such as sales, property, and income tax exemptions at the state level. The IRS points out that while most federal tax-exempt organizations are nonprofit organizations, organizing, as a nonprofit at the state level does not automatically grant you an exemption from federal income tax.

Another major difference between a profit and nonprofit business deals with the treatment of the profits. With a for-profit business, the owners and shareholders receive the profits. With a nonprofit, any money that is left after the organization has paid its bills is put back into the organization. Some types of nonprofits can receive contributions that are tax deductible to the individual who contributes to the organization. Keep in mind that nonprofits are organized to provide some benefit to the public.

Nonprofits are incorporated under the laws of the state in which they are established. To receive federal tax-exempt status, the organization must apply with the IRS. Two applications are required. First, you must request an Employer Identification Number (EIN) and then apply for recognition of exemption by filing Form 1023 (Charitable Organizations) or 1024 (Other Tax-Exempt Organizations), with the necessary filing fee.

The IRS identifies the several types of nonprofit organizations by the tax code by which they qualify for exempt status. One of the most common forms is 501(c)(3), which is set up to do charitable, educational, scientific, religious, and literary work. This includes a wide range of organizations, from continuing education centers to outpatient clinics and hospitals.

The IRS also mandates that there are certain activities tax-exempt organizations cannot engage in if they want to keep their exempt status. For example, a section 501(c)(3) organization cannot intervene in political campaigns.

Remember, nonprofits still must pay employment taxes, but in some states, they may be exempt from paying sales tax. Check with your state to make sure you understand how nonprofit status is treated in your area. In addition, nonprofits may be hit with unrelated business income tax. This is regular income from a trade or business that is not related to the charitable purpose. An exempt organization with $1,000 or more of gross income from an unrelated business must file Form 990-T and pay tax on the income.

If your nonprofit has revenues of more than $25,000 a year, you must file an annual report (Form 990) with the IRS. Form 990-EZ is a shortened version of 990 and is designed for use by small exempt organizations with total assets at the end of the year of less than $25,000. Form 990 asks you to provide information on the organization's income, expenses and staff salaries that exceed $50,000. You also may have to comply with a similar state requirement.

Last one! Certified B Corporations are businesses that meet the highest standards of verified social and environmental performance, public transparency, and legal accountability to balance profit and purpose. B Corps form a community of leaders and drive a global movement of people using business as a force for good. Ex. Ben & Jerry's

Requirements of Pending B Corp Status: Meet the legal accountability requirement for B Corp Certification; Complete and submit a prospective B Impact Assessment, Sign the Pending B Corp Agreement, and pay a one-time fee of $500.

GLOSSARY

AN

ALPHABETICAL

LIST

OF

DEFINITIONS

A

Acceptance – The offeree indicates their willingness to enter into the contract and to abide by the terms and conditions agreed upon. It is essential in forming a contract. There are many forms of acceptance, i.e., can be done orally, in writing, or by conduct.

Adjudicated (adjudged) Incompetent – A person who is declared incompetent by a court of law now lacks the legal capacity to enter into any enforceable contract.

Age of Majority – In general, this is the "legal" contractual age when a person is considered an adult. In most states, it is 18 years of age.

Alternative Dispute Resolution (ADR) – ADR is any legal procedure agreed to by the parties in a dispute, to avoid litigation, i.e., going to court. ADR is viewed as a forum for a better solution to meet the needs of the parties. (See Arbitration, Mediation).

Answer – In a lawsuit, the party must respond to the allegations and claims being made, and/or deny them. (See complaint).

Arbitration – This is an example of an ADR method where one or more people will hear a dispute between the parties and render a decision. This decision is binding.

Assent – The act of agreeing and shows the willingness to enter into the contract.

Assignment – This is a legal term that occurs when one party in a contract transfers rights, property, or other benefits to a third party. The assignor (giver) transfers to the assignee, (receiver), and a new contract is created.

Auctions – Auctions are an example of a "special offer." The bids made are offers to enter into an enforceable contract. Two types of auctions exist: Auctions without reserve (the highest bid must be accepted by the seller), and Auctions with reserve. (A specific price must be met, or the seller can reject the bid).

B

Bids – offers made in auctions. (See auction).

Bilateral Contract – This is where both parties mutually agree to the terms and conditions of the contract. It is formed when the parties both agree when the offeror initiates the contract, and the offeree accepts.

Blue Laws – A state or local law that bans certain commercial activities on a Sunday. Blue laws have dated back to the colonial period of American history. They are referred to as "Sunday Closing Laws." (See Sabbath laws).

Breach of Contract – A breach of contract occurs when one or both parties in the contract fail to perform their duties or obligations under the contract. This happens more often when one party, (the non-breaching party), has fulfilled its duties and the other (the breaching party), has not.

Breach of Warranty – This occurs when the goods fail to meet the standards made by the seller.

C

Capacity – The capacity to enter into a contract is defined as the parties having the ability to understand the contract, and to have agreed to its terms. (See competent). It is required for all contracts to be enforceable.

Cease and Desist Letter – (stop harassment letter or a demand letter) – The purpose is to put an individual or a business on notice that they are engaging in some sort of activity that is believed to be causing harm, and if not stopped, legal action will be commenced. These letters are meant to serve as harsh warnings, but they do not have any immediate legal consequences.

Class Action Lawsuit – This type of case involves many people with the same issue or cause of action. It allows one lawsuit to be brought on behalf of many parties, ("the class"), instead of each one filing an individual case.

Common Law of Contracts – This is the law that is derived from judicial decisions, i.e., cases and the parties involved. It covers services provided under the contract. Common law in the United States is derived from England's Common law.

Complaint – This is the document that starts the case. It is filed by the party who is initiating the case, stating the cause of action, (what occurred), and what relief is being sought. (See answer).

Compensatory Damages – These monetary damages are awarded to compensate for the actual loss incurred by the non-breaching party. The damages must be proven and measurable against the loss or injury.

Competent – The competency to enter into a contract is defined as the parties having the ability to understand the contract, and to have agreed to its terms. (See capacity). It is required for all contracts to be enforceable.

Consequential Damages -These monetary damages are awarded because they are foreseeable due to the breach, i.e., if the breach had not occurred, these damages would not exist. Ex. Attorney fees/Court fees/Expert Witnesses.

Consideration – This is an essential and one of the most essential elements of contracts. A contract cannot exist without consideration. It is the legal exchange agreed upon by the parties, or a mutually agreed upon exchange of benefits, and is the reason the parties enter into a contract.

Consumer Expectation Test – This implied warranty of food is based on the following: what can a consumer reasonably expect to find in their food products, as compared to a foreign substance.

Contract – This is a mutual agreement between the parties that is enforceable by law. Every contract must meet the basic requirements or essential elements to be enforced.

Contrary to Public Policy – Basically, a contract is deemed contrary to public policy if it results in a negative impact on society, and/or can cause harm/injury to individuals. It is considered against the public good and can be very subjective.

Counterfeit – These products are fake or unauthorized replicas of real products. They are often produced with the intent to take advantage of the superior value of the imitated products.

Counteroffer – This is made by the offeree, which functions as a rejection of the original offer, and a new offer to enter into the contract. The original offer can no longer be accepted and the roles of the parties, (offeror and offeree), have changed. The counteroffer gives the original offeror three options: accept the counteroffer, reject it, or made a new one.

Copyright – (the right to copy) -This is the exclusive right given to an originator to print, publish, perform film, or record any literary artistic or musical material, and to authorize others do the same.

Courts of Limited Jurisdiction – The lowest level of the court system. These courts can only hear specific cases. Ex. Family court, Traffic Court. If applicable, the case involved would start here if it involved the specific issue.

Courts of General Jurisdiction – (Trial Courts) - These courts have the authority to hear and decide all cases brought before them. There are two types: Criminal and Civil. Each court can hear any criminal case brought before it or any civil case brought before it. If not, a specific issue (limited jurisdiction), then the case would start at this level of the court.

Court of Appeals – Appellate Courts – These courts may hear cases from the general jurisdiction level. Usually, it is to determine whether the general jurisdiction court was correct when the decision was made by the trial court, and if not, to grant an appeal.

Creditor Beneficiary – This type of beneficiary receives the benefit of the contract as a repayment for a debt when the party may default, not make payment. This is standard in many contracts such as credit cards, student loans, etc.

D

Damages – What the party seeks as compensation for loss or injury caused by a wrongful or willful act of another. The recovery of damages is the objective of most contract litigations.

Defenses (to enforcing a contract) – Defenses are reasons not to enforce a valid contract. The contract itself has met all the requirements, but there still may exist a reason for the contract not to be enforced.

Delegation – A delegation is a legal term that occurs when one party in a contract, transfers only the duties to a third party. The delegator (giver) transfers the duties to the delegatee, (receiver), but a new contract is not created. The original parties remain in privity of contract.

Design Patent – Any new, original, and ornamental design for an article of manufacture. A design patent only protects the appearance of the article.

Dilution – This occurs in trademarks that diminishes the capacity of a famous mark used to identify its goods or services. It lessens the "uniqueness" of the trademark.

Disaffirmance – This legal term refers to the right for one party to cancel a contract, i.e., that they will not be bound by the contract and have indicated this to the offeror. A minor has a right to disaffirm most contracts is often used in law.

Discharge of Performance – This occurs when one or both parties in a contract fail to perform their duties and/or obligations.

Disclaimers – The purpose here is to inform people that the liability may be limited depending on the terms of the contract. It is often found in activities that are considered "high risk," or warnings when using products. A disclaimer can also limit the liability for a breach when it is part of the contract and agreed upon between the parties.

Donee Beneficiary – This beneficiary receives the benefit of the contract that was made between two other parties. Technically, they are not a party to the contract. Ex. One who inherits under a will or life insurance policy. The donor (giver) ensures the benefit will be given to the donee (receiver).

Duress -In simple terms, duress is where the offending party uses threats of force/violence, and what is considered illegitimate (illegal), pressure to force the other party to enter a contract. Thus, overcoming the free will of the other party.

E

Emancipation – This is the legal process that gives minors many important rights, and the parental duty is terminated. It can be voluntary or involuntary.

Equitable Remedy – The purpose is the non-breaching party may not want monetary damages but is asking the court to cure or to fix the breach under the concepts of "fairness and justice."

Equity – The court will enforce a contract based on the concept of "fairness and justice." In other words, it would be unfair for one party to benefit and not the other.

Executory Contracts -The definition is that either one or both parties have not yet performed what was required under the contract. It is still considered "open," or not yet completed/finished and may take place at a future time.

Executed Contracts – Both parties have fully performed their duties/obligations under the contract. There is nothing remaining in the contract to be fulfilled.

Express Contracts - This is the easiest formation of contracts in which both parties agree to the terms. Either it can be declared orally, or in writing, or a combination of both, at the time the contract is entered into and made.

Express Warranty – An express warranty occurs when the seller makes a written or oral statement of fact relating to the goods being sold, and that the goods meet these standards, which are the benefit of the bargain. The warranty ensures that the goods will conform to the statement or promise made by the seller.

F – G

Fair Use – This legal doctrine is to promote freedom of expression by permitting the unlicensed use of intellectually protected works to be used under certain circumstances, without permission of the owner. Ex. Teaching.

Federal District Court – (Criminal and Civil) – This court has the authority to hear federal criminal cases and federal civil cases. Ex. A federal crime – violation of securities (stocks, etc.) such as insider knowledge. This is the lowest level of the federal court system.

Federal Court of Appeals – This is the highest federal court in the state. This court has the authority to hear cases from the federal district court, either criminal or civil.

Federal Registration – The registration of intellectual properties at this level grants more rights and protections for enforcement and infringement.

False Advertising – This consists of untrue or misleading information given to consumers to get them to purchase an item, or for them to visit their store. Those who make products must honestly present the products and services to the public.

Firm Offer Rule – A merchant makes a written offer and states that the offer will remain open for a specific time period, and then the merchant cannot revoke or amend the offer prior or during the time period stated.

First Amendment – The first Amendment guarantees certain freedoms such as religion, expression, assembly, and the right to petition the government. It guarantees freedom of expression by prohibiting the government from restricting the rights of the people to speak freely. It was part of the Bill of Rights and was added to the Constitution on December 15, 1791. However, there are exceptions to what is protected under the First Amendment.

Foreign Substance Test – This implied warranty is if the object found in the food is not naturally occurring (foreign to the food), then it is a breach, and the warranty is violated.

Fraud – Contract fraud occurs when a person knowingly and intentionally makes a false statement to have another party enter into the contract. It is intended to deceive and induce the party to enter into the contract that might not have otherwise agreed to enter. Fraud must involve an intentional lie of a material fact.

Frivolous – There is no legal significance and refers to a parties attempt to delay the case. Courts consider this as "bad faith," and may sanction the wrongdoer.

Gambling – A gambling contract is the act of exchanging valuables in a game, lottery, casino, etc. It varies from state to state. If the state approves, then gambling is considered a legal contract. If not approved, is an illegal contract.

Genuineness of Assent – This requirement is also known as a "genuine agreement and genuine assent." The party's agreement to enter into a legally enforceable contract is agreed upon, or assented to by the parties, with full knowledge of the contract and its requirements.

Goods – Goods are tangible and movable property from the seller to the buyer at the time of the sales contract. Thus, goods apply mostly to items that are manufactured because they can be transferred at the time of the sale. Another term for goods is "chattels."

H - I

Hierarchy of Courts – The levels of the court system, starting with the lowest level.

Illegality – In contracts, this concept indicates that the contract is unenforceable, even if all other requirements were met to form the contract, it would still not be enforced by the courts.

Implied Contracts -This contract may or may not exist based on the conduct and circumstances of the parties. It could be formed without the parties essentially agreeing to it. It is enforced by the courts depending on the conditions being met.

Implied-In-Fact Contract – This is one example of an implied contract and is a true contract. It is an enforceable contract based on the performance of the parties, expectations, and circumstances.

Implied-In-Law – This is another example of an implied contract but is not a true contract. The court is imposing a contract because it would be unfair to one party where there was performance, and a benefit was received. (See equity).

Implied Warranty – An implied warranty is where the product is fit for the purpose for which it is intended and is merchantable, i.e., conforms to the buyer's expectations.

Incidental Beneficiary – This type of beneficiary is a third party who may or may not benefit under the contract but is not intended to have any legal rights. Ex. Parents are intended to benefit under a will, which would also benefit their child, but the child is not intended to have any rights and cannot sue.

Incompetent – A person who is incompetent lacks the legal capacity to enter into an enforceable contract.

Infancy Doctrine – This rule protects minors, which states that a minor has an absolute right to disaffirm most contracts entered with an adult, any time prior to reaching the age of majority, or a reasonable time thereafter.

Infringement – This occurs when there is an unauthorized violation or a breach.

Injunction – This is a court order requiring a person to stop a specific action. In court, an injunction granted would take place immediately upon issuance.

Impossibility of Performance – This doctrine states the circumstances whereby one party can be released from a contract due to unforeseen circumstances that render performance impossible. In other words, there was literally no possible way for the party to perform its duties.

Insane – The definition of insanity is the inability to differentiate "right from wrong." It is most often used in criminal law. In contract law, the capacity of the parties is required. (A higher standard than insanity).

Intended Beneficiary – This party has been explicitly named in the contract as one that is intended from the onset to receive the benefits associated with the execution of the contract.

Intangible Consideration – The legal exchange between the parties consists of the following: forbearance (giving up something not legally obligated to do or abstaining from doing something), which is a legal detriment. (Incurring a loss).

Intellectual Property – This refers to creations of the minds, such as inventions, literary and artistic works, designs, symbols, and names and images used in commerce.

Intellectual Property Rights (IPR) – This refers to the legal rights given to the inventor or creator to protect their invention or creation for a specific time period.

Intoxication – The intoxicated person has consumed enough drugs/alcohol to cause impairment in judgment so that they could not understand the legal ramifications of entering a contract.

J - K

Jurisdiction - The concept of can have varied meanings depending on how the term is used. It is an important concept in law as it refers to the legal authority of the courts to act. The most effective definition would be as follows: "The authority of the courts, to hear a case (the ability to listen to the case), make a decision, and ultimately, to be able to enforce the decision."

Knock-off – These products are those that copy or imitate the physical appearance of other products but do not copy the brand name or logo of a trademark. A "knock-off" in fashion is the act or instance of knocking off an unlicensed copy of something, especially fashion clothing, intended to be sold at a lower price than the original.

L

Lanham Act – The purpose here is to protect trademarks and will offer protection against false advertising. It prevents other companies from using the logo, design, symbol, work, or phrase used by another business entity.

Legal Remedy - This is also referred to as judicial relief or a judicial remedy. The purpose here is to cure or fix a breach that has occurred to the non-breaching party, the party who has performed their duty or obligation.

Liquidated Damages – These monetary damages are agreed upon in advance and are included in the terms of the contract. In essence, a liquidated damages clause eliminates the need to have a court resolution of a contractual breach and dispute. It is a provision that allows for the payment of a pre-determined specified sum should one of the parties breach the contract.

Litigation – The process of bringing, maintaining, and defending a lawsuit, (case) in court.

Litigators – Attorneys who are usually in court trying to resolve a case. Not all attorneys are litigators, meaning do not go to court at all.

M-N-O

Mailbox Rule –The mailbox rule (also called the posting rule) is a common law concept that states an offer is considered accepted upon dispatch. (sent). This indicates that acceptance would be effective once it is mailed in the post office, with the presumption that it would be delivered.

Manifestation of assent – the offeree must demonstrate that they have accepted and agreed to the terms of the contract.

Mediation – This is an example of an ADR method where one or more persons will hear a dispute between the parties and make suggestions for resolution. Unlike arbitration, the decision is not binding.

Meeting of Minds – A meeting of minds is synonymous with "mutual agreement, mutual assent." It indicates that the parties were both on the "same page" when they entered the contract. It is an essential requirement for the contract to be enforceable.

Merchant – A merchant is defined as a person who deals in goods, (seller and buyer), or who has more knowledge and experience than the average consumer does.

Miller Test – This test was developed from a case consisting of a 3-prong test to determine whether a work is obscene. All three prongs must be met for the work to be considered obscene. (See Miller v The State of California (June 21, 1973)).

Minor – In most states, minors (under the age of 18 years old), lack the capacity to make a contract. Thus, when a minor signs a contract, the minor may or may not execute the terms of the contract. There are a few contractual exceptions. (See necessities).

Mirror Image Rule – This common law rule is important, as it requires "unequivocal acceptance." The offeror mandates the terms for acceptance, and it legally defines when a contract becomes legally binding and enforceable.

Mitigation – This principle states that the party who has suffered a loss from the breach of the contract, (the non-breaching party), must take action to try to avoid or reduce the loss or damages suffered, if it is reasonable to do so under the circumstances.

Mixed Sale – This occurs in one transaction where there are goods which fall under the Uniform Commercial Code, and services that fall under Common Law. The area of law used will be decided on the predominant part of the contract.

Mutual Mistake - A mutual mistake occurs when both parties are mistaken, or in error, as to the subject matter or the terms that are contained in the contractual agreement. Here, the parties are at cross-purposes, i.e., there is no meeting of the minds.

Mutual Rescission – Both parties can mutually agree to rescind and or, terminate (end), the contract.

Necessities – (Necessaries of Life) – In most states, a minor will be held responsible for certain contracts like food, clothing, shelter, education, medical care, etc. A necessity for a contract might be formed depending on the circumstances involved even if not the standard.

Negligence – This occurs when the party has a duty, the party has breached the duty, and this breach has caused a direct injury or harm to another.

Nominal Damages – These damages may be awarded to the party when there is a breach of their legal rights, but no actual monetary loss or injury has occurred, or can be proven. It is based on the principle that the party wants the right to be recognized since a breach has occurred.

Objective Theory of Contracts – This important theory in contracts decides that an agreement made between the parties is enforceable in the opinion of the "reasonable person," who is not a party to the contract. It is the standard used depending on where the case is being heard. (See Reasonable Person Standard).

Offer – The offer must contain all the essential terms (see terms) by the offeror to the offeree when initiating a contract. It is the process to start the formation of an enforceable contract. Ex. First: an offer is made containing all the relevant terms, and Second: whether the other party agrees to accept or not.

Offeror – The party who initiates and has the intent to make an offer. This is the beginning process of entering into a legally binding contract formation.

Offeree – The party who can accept/or not accept the offer initiated by the offeror.

P-Q

Parental Duty – Parents have a duty to provide their child/children with the necessities of life, until they reach the age of majority. This age varies from state to state. Exception: See Emancipation.

Parol (word) Evidence Rule – An important rule in contracts where the written and signed contract is presumed to be the final agreement between the parties. Therefore, the purpose is to prevent a party from introducing any written or oral statements that may contradict the final contract. In other words, if it is not in the final agreement, it is inadmissible.

Patent -The exclusive property right granted to an inventor for a specific time period in exchange for the complete disclosure of the invention.

Personal Jurisdiction – The authority of the courts to make and enforce a decision over the parties in the case, i.e., the plaintiff and the defendant. There must be a notion of fairness – what connection do the parties have to the state and what benefits do they get which allows the courts to have personal jurisdiction over them? It is based on the following:

1. The parties reside in the state.

2. The parties do business in the state – Ex. Minimum contacts.

3. The parties' own real estate in the state – In rem jurisdiction.

4. There was an occurrence in the state.

Personal Property – This consists of items such as cars, clothing, computers, etc.

Privity of Contract – This doctrine is based on a common law principle, which indicates that only the parties to a contract are intended to benefit under the contract, and have rights, duties, and the ability to sue. Thus, this doctrine excludes any party not in privity of contract to have any rights or benefits.

Promises – Generally, a promise is not binding in a contract. There are certain circumstances where a promise may be enforceable in a contract. (See promissory estoppel).

Promissory Estoppel – A promise may be enforceable in a contract if the person to whom the promise is made has reasonably acted upon reliance of the promise, which causes that person to suffer a detriment. (loss)

Punitive Damages – This type of damage is considered punishment, i.e., to punish the wrongdoer, the party who breached. They are awarded at the discretion of the court when the behavior is found to be especially harmful or damaging to the other party. It is also meant as a warning that this type of behavior will not be tolerated.

R

Ratification – A party ratifies a contract when they accept the benefit, thus making the contract legally enforceable. Basically, it is the acceptance and approval of the contract.

Real Property – The definition is land, homes, condominiums, buildings, or property that is attached to the land. (non-movable).

Reformation – This is the court's equitable power to modify a contract to reflect the true intent or value of the contract when some error has occurred. The court can rewrite the contract to what is determined to be fair and just.

Reasonable Person Standard (RPS) – An important theory that determines whether an "objective person," as opposed to a "subjective person," would determine that an enforceable contract exists between the parties. This standard is applied in many areas of law.

Restatement of Contracts – The Restatement of Contracts is a legal treatise (encyclopedia) informing about general principles and definitions of contract law. It was written by legal scholars as a methodology to "restate" terms and definitions used.

Restitution – A party is returned to the "status quo," as if the contract has not been performed. The party would receive back the full value they were given in the contractual exchange.

Restoration – A party would receive back the current value in the contractual exchange.

Revocation – This term refers to the offeror who can cancel or revoke the offer being made. The purpose of the withdrawal of the offer is that the offeree can no longer accept it.

Reward – A reward is considered a "special offer." It requires the offeree to have knowledge about the offer and to perform the requested act.

Risk of Loss – This term is used to determine which party will bear the risk of loss for damage occurring to goods after the sale has been completed. Once the buyer takes possession, the risk of loss passes from the seller to the buyer. The buyer has a right to inspect the goods before acceptance.

S

Sabbath Laws – These laws regulate or prohibit commercial activities on Sundays, which was the "Lord's Day." It may vary depending on the religion as to what is considered a Sabbath day.

Sale – The contract between the seller and the buyer as the title (ownership) is being transferred.

Secondary Meaning – In trademarks, an additional non-distinct meaning is acquired through its commercial use in the minds of the consumers. Ex. A specific color.

Silence as Acceptance – Generally, a contract cannot be accepted by silence. However, there are certain exceptions where silence can be deemed as acceptance, depending on the parties and the circumstances involved.

Specific Performance – This remedy is where the court orders a party to perform the "act" as closely as possible because monetary damages are not adequate to fix or cure the harm incurred.

Standing to Sue – An important concept where the party/parties bringing the case to court must have a significant connection to the case at hand. Ex. The parties were injured and has sufficient legal interest to participate in the case.

State Registration – The registration of intellectual properties at this level may only grant certain rights and protections.

State Supreme Court – This is the highest state court. Their authority is exclusive for appeals of issues that were not decided by the Appellate Court.

Statute of Limitations – The maximum period (time allowed), in which a party can bring a case to court. This varies depending on the type of case and the state involved. Cases not met within this time frame will be barred (stopped) from being heard.

Statute of Frauds (Law of Frauds) – This statute requires certain contracts to be in writing to enforced, and therefore, cannot be done orally. The purpose is to be clear on the requirements of the contract as they may be complex. Six well-known contracts fall under this category.

   Ex. Marriage, Contracts longer than one year, Estates (wills, trusts), Land (real estate), Guarantor (agreeing to pay for the debts of a third party), and the Sales of goods that exceed $500.

Strict Product Liability – There is an expectation that all products are safe. Under this theory, anyone involved in the chain of distribution of a product may be held accountable if there is any injury to the consumers, even if the consumer may be at fault. This applies to the manufacturer, wholesaler, retailer, distributor, etc. Everyone has a duty to make sure all products in the marketplace are safe.

Subject matter Jurisdiction – The authority of the courts to hear and decide cases based on the ability of the applicable subject matter at issue. Ex. A bankruptcy court only has the authority to hear bankruptcy cases due to the subject matter. Ex. Family court will only hear family-related issues, i.e., child custody, support.

T

Tangible Consideration – The legal exchange between the parties consists of one of the following: money, property, or services.

Terms – The basic essential elements of every contract that are extremely specific and definite. They are determined by the parties entering into the contract. These terms outline who the parties are, what they are seeking, payment, etc. Most terms are standard but can be made to specify the needs of the parties to be clear as to what has been agreed by both.

Third Party Rights – A third party is a beneficiary who receives a benefit (rights), from a contract made between two other parties. Therefore, the third party is not in privity of contract, but is intended to benefit from the onset of the contract being created.

Title – This indicates who the owner is.

Trade Dress – This represents the design and shape of the materials in which a product is packaged. Also called product configuration, representing the design and shape of the product itself.

Trademark – This can be any word, phrase, symbol, design, or a combination thereof, that can identify the origin of a business, or the goods, products or services affiliated with that business.

Trade Secret – Information that is intended to be kept confidential and effort must be made to do so. This includes customer lists and manufacturing processes. There is economic value in the information.

<u>U - V</u>

Unconscionable – This applies in contracts when the contract is considered so unfair/unjust that it "shocks the conscience of the court." It is when one party has an advantage and is using it against the other parties' weakness/weaknesses, rendering the contract to be oppressive to one party at the time the contract is formed, possible overcoming free will.

Undue Influence – This occurs when the parties are in a special relationship, and because of that relationship, they are taking advantage of the other party's mental, physical, or emotional weakness, to enter into a contract.

Unfair Competition – This occurs when one is using illegal, deceptive, and fraudulent selling practices that harm consumers or other businesses to gain a competitive advantage in the market. Acts done by a seller to confuse or deceive the public with the intent to acquire a larger portion of the market.

Uniform Commercial Code (UCC) – The UCC, as the title suggests, has as its primary purposed to make business codes (laws) more consistent (uniform) in commerce across the United States. Each state has its own UCC.

Unilateral Contract – This contract can only be accepted by performance, i.e., the party does the act requested and will be formed when the act is started. There is no guarantee to the offeror that the offeree will accept/perform what is requested.

Unilateral Mistake – A unilateral mistake occurs when only one party is mistaken, or in error, as to the subject matter or the terms that are contained in the contractual agreement.

U.S. Supreme Court (SCOTUS) – This is the highest court in the United States. "EQUAL JUSTICE UNDER THE LAW" – these are the words written above the main entrance to the court. It has the authority to hear all cases and controversies as the final arbiter of the law. The purpose here is to ensure that the people are promised equal justice under the law. It also functions to maintain the Constitution.

Usury – A contract is considered "usurious," when it is an agreement between the parties where the interest rate imposed is higher than is permitted by law.

Venue – The specific location in which a case is brought and to be heard. A change of venue can be requested. The court must have jurisdiction to hear the case.

Valid Legal Controversy – The subject matter of the case must be important enough for the court to hear the case. If not, the case may be considered "frivolous," and dismissed by the court. (See "frivolous.")

Voidable Contract – The parties may have an option not to perform, i.e., conduct the terms of the contract. It is an enforceable contract.

Void Contract – The contract is not enforceable by the courts and has no legal value. It may have been void from the onset of the contract or could become void after the formation if laws change regarding contracts. Ex. The essence (purpose) of the contract becomes illegal.

W-X-Y-Z

Warranty – In general, a warranty is a promise, assurance, or a statement made by the seller regarding the existence or accuracy of specific facts as the condition, quality, or nature of the goods. The warranty is the reason the consumer has entered into the contract. This is known as the benefit of bargain, i.e., why the consumer entered the contract.

-THE END-

Made in the USA
Middletown, DE
19 October 2023

41102890R00080